$\frac{8}{14}$

APR · 2011

THE EXCEPTIONAL PRESENTER
GOES VIRTUAL

**TAKE COMMAND OF YOUR MESSAGE,
CREATE AN "IN-PERSON" EXPERIENCE AND
CAPTIVATE ANY REMOTE AUDIENCE**

TIMOTHY J. KOEGEL

GREENLEAF
BOOK GROUP PRESS

Published by Greenleaf Book Group Press
Austin, Texas
www.gbgpress.com

Distributed by Greenleaf Book Group LLC

For ordering information or special discounts for bulk purchases, please contact Greenleaf Book Group LLC at PO Box 91869, Austin, TX 78709, 512.891.6100.

Design and composition by Greenleaf Book Group LLC and Alex Head
Cover design by Greenleaf Book Group LLC
Illustrations by Tom Holtkamp

Publisher's Cataloging-in-Publication Data
(Prepared by The Donohue Group, Inc.)
Koegel, Timothy J.
   The exceptional presenter goes virtual : take command of your message, create an "in-person" experience, and captivate any remote audience / Timothy J. Koegel.—1st ed.
     p. ; cm.
   ISBN: 978-1-60832-046-2
   1. Business presentations. 2. Business communication. 3. Business presentations—Audio-visual aids. 4. Business communication—Computer networks. I. Title.
HF5718.22 .K64 2010
658.4/52/0285   2010929433

Part of the Tree Neutral™ program, which offsets the number of trees consumed in the production and printing of this book by taking proactive steps, such as planting trees in direct proportion to the number of trees used: www.treeneutral.com

TreeNeutral™

Printed in the United States of America on acid-free paper

10 11 12 13 14 15   10 9 8 7 6 5 4 3 2 1

First Edition

To Chris, Vic, Steve and Theresa.

To everyone who helped me organize, research and write this book.

CONTENTS

KEEP IT ENGAGING

FROM THE AUTHOR

THE TECHNIQUES IN THIS BOOK are designed to enable you to feel confident about presenting in any virtual presentation setting using any technology. If the technology changes, it doesn't matter—and you shouldn't worry. The skills outlined in this book do not depend on the technology. They are fundamental communication techniques that can be applied to any virtual presentation. The challenges of presenting to a remote audience are often more daunting than presenting to an in-person audience. Virtual presentations are becoming more and more a part of our everyday communication. If you want to maximize your communication impact in the coming years then becoming an exceptional virtual presenter is not an option; it is a necessity.

The Exceptional Presenter Goes Virtual is a quick read and a quick reference. Every page of this book is relevant and every technique is actionable. You will be able to apply the techniques in this book immediately.

Visit www.theexceptionalpresenter.com for tips, suggestions and worksheets that will help to make all of your presentations exceptional.

CHAPTER 1
OPPORTUNITY AWAITS

THE NUMBER OF VIRTUAL PRESENTATIONS is growing exponentially. Improved technology, combined with the "Perfect Storm" of the heightened security risk and travel hassle since 9/11, the seemingly ever-present threat of and exposure to the latest pandemic and the global financial meltdown, has elevated virtual presentations as a practical, safe, efficient and cost-effective means of communicating with employees, customers, prospects, users and coworkers.

The rise in the frequency, versatility and availability of online communication has opened a huge cyber door of opportunity for those who take the steps to improve their virtual presentation proficiency.

If you already possess strong in-person presentation skills, this book will help you to transfer those skills to the virtual presentation world. If your in-person presentation skills are less than exceptional, this book offers you a second chance to elevate your communication prowess in a different venue—the virtual world. An additional bonus comes from using the techniques in this book: by learning how to organize and deliver virtual presentations with greater clarity and impact, you will simultaneously improve your in-person skills.

If you forget everything else you read in this book, remember these three principles:

1) A successful *virtual meeting* is a series of exceptional presentations, fused together by seamless transitions and delivered with passion and professionalism.

2) Your virtual presentation must be relevant, or it will be ignored. It must be engaging, or it will be forgotten. It must keep moving, or it will be abandoned.

3) You are the messenger. Technology can provide an endless supply of gadgets and bells and whistles to enhance your presentation, but ultimately it is your message and your delivery that will move the audience to take action.

"The trouble with the future is that it usually arrives before we're ready for it."

—Arnold Glasgow

THE FUTURE IS NOW

The use of online communication now extends far beyond the business meeting to almost any means of communication (for example, medical examinations, trade shows, conferences, interviews, tours, product demonstrations and training, among others). The following list appeared in my book *The Exceptional Presenter* and was included to illustrate the many places in which we can find ourselves presenting. Look at the list and check the venues in which we can now communicate virtually:

☐ Proposals	☐ Prospecting calls
☐ Job interviews	☐ Customer service
☐ Negotiating	☐ Training
☐ IPO road shows	☐ Radio or TV appearances
☐ Fund-raising	☐ Social functions
☐ Client reviews	☐ Banquets
☐ Casual conversations	☐ Brainstorming sessions
☐ Recruiting	☐ Interviewing candidates
☐ Board meetings	☐ Mentoring
☐ Talking to your children	☐ Sharing your vision
☐ Arguing	☐ Debating
☐ Gossiping	☐ Teaching
☐ Sales meetings	☐ Staff meetings
☐ Voice mail	☐ Networking
☐ Phone conversations	☐ Instructing others
☐ Counseling	☐ Cold calls
☐ Keynote speeches	☐ Introducing others
☐ Team presentations	☐ Product introductions
☐ Key account meetings	☐ Q&A sessions
☐ Hosting an event	☐ Reading at services
☐ Luncheons	☐ Questioning clients
☐ Selling products	☐ Updating superiors
☐ Coaching	☐ Talking with spouse
☐ Talking with peers	☐ Working convention booths

We can check every venue on the list. We have reached the point in time when, by simply carrying a camera or a microphone, we can present our information, ideas, solutions and data to someone, somewhere in the world.

As the technology evolves, we will find ourselves communicating virtually much more frequently. We will be asked to lead or participate in a range of remote communication settings.

Therefore, we need to become better virtual presenters.

UNDERSTAND THE BARRIERS, OR THEY WILL TRIP YOU UP

The reality is that when it comes to presenting, most people fall well short of their potential. They don't learn how to craft a clear, concise and compelling message. They don't develop effective presentation delivery skills that reflect their level of competence and professionalism. And they are unaware of what it takes to keep an audience engaged and involved in a presentation.

How can anyone expect to achieve exceptional results with less than exceptional skills? And taking those skills and placing them in a virtual setting poses additional challenges and complexities to the planning and delivery of your presentations such as

- Presenting to silent or muted audiences.
- Presenting to invisible audiences.
- Receiving little or no feedback or input from the audience.
- Connecting participants and keeping them connected.
- Navigating a set of web tools that a gamer would have difficulty operating.
- Presenting to a remote audience that is probably surfing the web, emailing, texting, tweeting, catching-up on work or otherwise multitasking during your presentation.

The multitasking alone is enough to dilute the impact of your message. In some organizations, online meetings are viewed as an opportunity to *get other stuff done*. An August 2009 *Forbes Insights* article titled "Business Meetings—The Case for Face-to-Face" reported findings of a survey of 750 senior business executives. Fifty-eight percent of the participants admitted that they "frequently" surf the web, check their email, read unrelated material and handle other ancillary work during digital meetings.

One executive laughed as he told me, "I swear I heard a toilet flush during my presentation." Perhaps he could consider that action an evaluation of his presentation.

HOW THIS BOOK WILL HELP YOU

Unless you bury your head in the sand or hide away on some deserted island, you are going to be involved in more online presentations going forward. Virtual presentations command an extra level of detail and planning, a more assertive delivery style and superior resourcefulness to keep your audience engaged. In order to thrive in this new digital frontier, you must possess a systematic process for planning and executing your virtual presentations.

Until now there hasn't been a resource that provided virtual presenters with a systematic method of preparing for and delivering online presentations. Most of the best practices I have seen are a collection of suggestions for using the bells and whistles that the various online meeting options offer. These best practices include suggestions such as "Be interactive, dynamic and engaging," "Ask questions," "Use the tools," "Smile with your voice," and "Have fun."

I agree that we should smile with our voice, and we should have fun. Where these best practices fall short is that they offer few, if any, suggestions as to how to make your online presentations dynamic, engaging, interactive and fun. They don't address the most basic elements, including how to plan and sequence your

THINGS TO DO TODAY

8 AM	MEET SERGEI IN MOSCOW (WEBINAR)
9 AM	CLIENT REVIEW: LONDON (VIDEO CONFERENCE)
10AM	Q+A WITH NY REPS (TELEPRESENCE)
NOON	BREAKFAST W/JENNY IN LA (WEBCAST)
1:30PM	GOLF - FRONT NINE
	CALL KEVIN IN SYDNEY (PHONE)
	- BACK NINE *** CLUB RECORD 71
6:30PM	LAURA'S PIANO RECITAL (IN PERSON)

Steve was thrilled that his travel time and his golf scores dropped simultaneously.

virtual presentation or how to make the presentation feel like an in-person experience. Asking questions is one way to get the audience involved, but there are many additional ways to engage the audience that are never spelled out.

The Exceptional Presenter Goes Virtual is all about how to do it. It provides the process for planning and executing high-impact virtual presentations. The purpose of this book is to make virtual presentations less daunting by changing the way you approach each presentation. This book will break a virtual presentation into its components and then provide techniques, skills and practice methods that enable you to improve each skill incrementally. The incremental improvement of multiple skills leads to significant overall improvement in effectiveness and consistency.

Once you are competent at applying these techniques, you will be able to use them in ANY virtual communication environment.

> **This book is not about the technology. It's about how to organize and deliver your message using the technology.**

The Exceptional Presenter Goes Virtual is organized into three segments.

Segment 1: Keep it relevant

Segment 2: Keep it engaging

Segment 3: Keep it moving

Keep it relevant

Your virtual presentation must be relevant, or it will be ignored. What must be relevant? Everything.

- The purpose
- The topics
- The message
- The agenda, timing and flow
- The technology you choose
- The participants and their role in the presentation

Keep it engaging

Your virtual presentation must be engaging, or it will be forgotten. Every aspect of your virtual presentation should engage your audience. Make your presentation more interesting than anything that might distract your participants.

- Be resourceful. The same old same old doesn't work here.
- Start with the most interesting topic.
- Grab the attention of your audience with a dynamic and professional delivery.
- Involve members of the audience early and often.
- Don't fly solo.
- Create an in-person look and feel using more effective camera placement, lighting, surroundings and background.
- Use stories, examples, humor, visuals, video, sound and music.
- Make it fun.

Keep it moving

Your virtual presentation must keep moving, or it will be abandoned. Do not waste time. *Drag* is a four-letter word in this environment.

- Create smooth and efficient transitions and handoffs.
- Eliminate the irrelevant.
- Manage the clock.
- Practice your delivery and practice using the tools.

The *Exceptional Presenter Goes Virtual* will also provide guidance for

- Following up with your participants.
- Eliminating awkward moments: uncomfortable silence, humor where you hear no response, lag time during conversations, refusal of participants to speak up, stepping on each other's words and technology malfunctions.

- Choosing to go virtual, to present in person or to use a combination of the two.

- Deciding whether or not to record your virtual presentation or meeting.

The layout of this book is structured to be a quick read and a quick reference. It will not bog you down with theory. Every technique is pertinent and actionable. This is not a directory of online options for conducting your virtual presentations. It will not tell you which button to push for the various online tools. That's what IT departments are for. They can address your particular technology issue directly.

Researching and writing this book has been an exciting experience. Virtual presentations are creating a world in which our presentation reach is unlimited.

Presenting to an in-person audience is difficult. Presenting to a remote audience is difficult squared, unless you have a process.

It will not be long before you find yourself sitting at a conference table surrounded by the CEOs of eight of your biggest customers. You are assigned the task of persuading them to purchase your new and improved product. These executives have been beamed in from across the globe in the form of holograms. You have the latest and greatest technology for the presentation at your fingertips. It's time for the presentation to begin.

Even with all of the remarkable technology that makes the meeting possible, you still have to conduct the meeting. You still have to persuade your audience. The technology can't do it for you. You have to make your presentation relevant, you have to keep your information engaging, and you have to keep it moving.

CHAPTER 2
VIRTUAL PRESENTATIONS ARE ANYTHING BUT NEW

THE ONSLAUGHT OF AVAILABLE TECHNOLOGY for virtual presentations is both awe inspiring and somewhat intimidating. The technology and additional complexities it presents can be overwhelming. We are now being asked more frequently to use this technology, which was formerly the domain of trained professionals.

Fear not. The art of delivering presentations to remote audiences is anything but new. After all, radio and television have been delivering information to remote audiences for decades. Most of the United States has had commercial radio stations since the early 1920s and television stations since about 1940.

LEARN BY WATCHING THE PROFESSIONALS

Radio and television provide us with a never-ending supply of ideas for improving our online communication. Professionals in these industries face many of the same challenges that we face when we conduct virtual presentations. They present to remote audiences. Except in limited cases, they present to invisible and silent audiences. They can't see or hear the physical reactions of the audience. They can't make eye contact with them or see their facial expressions. They receive little to no feedback, other than an occasional email comment or question via Skype, text message or phone call. They assume that their audience is multitasking during the broadcast (for example, having dinner, driving, playing with the kids or cleaning the house). They operate within tight time constraints, and they have an enormous amount of competition vying for the attention of their audience members.

Broadcasting executives are keenly aware of what they are competing against. Their existence depends on understanding and overcoming the challenges they face. Only by executing their craft exceedingly well do they keep their jobs and stay on the air. If we pay close attention to what they're doing and how they're doing it, we can apply some of their techniques to make our virtual presentations more relevant, more engaging and more efficient.

For the next 30 days, as you watch and listen to television and radio, make note of how your favorite programs are organized, how the personalities interact, how the program moves through segments and topics and how the talent transitions from person to person and from segment to segment. Note the techniques they use to keep you from changing the channel. Observe the level of energy and enthusiasm of the talent and how efficient they are with their time. Watch programs that most reflect the interaction that occurs during your meetings. The techniques applied by talk shows, newscasts and documentaries will provide more practical delivery techniques than sitcoms and reality TV shows will.

There are some blatantly obvious differences between your virtual presentations and those of most radio and television programs. They have high-paid production teams developing each program. Chances are, you don't. They use $80,000 high-definition cameras and $70,000 editing equipment. Chances are, you don't. They have professional makeup and wardrobe consultants. You wish you did, but chances are, you don't.

Don't sweat it.

Life is not broadcast quality, so don't expect your virtual presentations to be.

Some of the most engaging and impactful video presentations have been produced without the bells, the whistles and the expensive equipment. These productions are impactful because the information is interesting and the people delivering the information are passionate. Good cameras and lighting help. The sound quality of any presentation is important. But it is the structure of the message and the quality of the delivery that create the impact.

Don't underestimate the similarities between radio and television broadcasts and your online presentations. Don't pass up an opportunity to learn from these two examples. By examining how it is done in broadcasting, we can pick up a plethora of techniques that will make our virtual presentations better.

Be thorough in your planning, focused on your audience and stingy with your time.

The following are *NBC Nightly News* archived segments that serve as excellent examples of the organization, content, timing, transition statements and flow of a news story. Notice the efficiency of each segment.

Time elapsed:

Start	Brian Williams (BW) "Good evening, while few people were willing to say it out loud . . ."
:16	Transition to full screen visual of jobs graph (BW voice-over)
:35	Transition: Back to BW on full screen
:43	Split screen showing reporters Savannah Guthrie (SG) and Miguel Almaguer (MA). "We begin with our White House correspondent Savannah Guthrie at the White House, Savannah good evening."
:51	Full screen of Savannah Guthrie (SG). "Good evening, Brian, they tried to put the best . . ."
1:03	Video of UPS workers, SG voice-over
1:08	Video of UPS control center, SG voice-over
1:14	Video of unemployment line, SG voice-over and animated graph
1:23	Video of President Obama walking toward a lectern
1:37	Quote from President Obama :10 seconds
1:47	Video of President Obama, SG voice-over
1:52	Graph of job loss numbers, SG voice-over

1:59	Video of a worker at a computer followed by a chart of job numbers, SG voice-over
2:11	Quote from White House Economic Advisor :07 seconds
2:18	Video of factory workers, SG voice-over
2:25	Quote from CNBC financial expert :07 seconds
2:32	Video of office space "For Lease" sign, SG voice-over
2:41	Quote from an economist :11 seconds
2:52	Live shot of SG standing in front of the White House for final comments. SG's transition statement back to BW, "But first Brian, they've got to get their health care."
3:07	END of segment

Here is another report that demonstrates the network's desire to get the audience involved using web tools.

Start with a split screen of BW and Nancy Snyderman, M.D.

:07	BW, "Dr. Nancy Snyderman is our NBC News, Chief Medical Editor. Nancy is with us from our home studios back in New York, and Nancy, our first question comes to us from Margaret . . ." Margaret's Live Chat question is posted on the screen. BW reads it out loud.
:29	Dr. Nancy's response on full screen
:50	End of answer BW, "Our next question comes to us via Skype." The lady on the video asks her question. Dr. Nancy full screen shot. She answers the question in 22 seconds.
1:32	Split screen of BW and a question emailed from a viewer. BW reads the email question.

1:45   BW, "What about it, Nancy?"

2:07   End of Nancy's answer.

BW and Nancy chat for 20 seconds, and the segment ends at 2:27

To think that your virtual presentation or meeting can compare to the *NBC Nightly News* is unrealistic. The point here is to demonstrate how fast and efficient newscasts are. They don't allow drag or down time. They use everything they have to make each segment relevant and visually appealing and engaging.

Reflect for a moment about the virtual presentations and meetings you have recently participated in or conducted. Compare the level of planning, efficiency and delivery of those meetings to the way the professionals use time, topics, talent and tools to plan and deliver a newscast. You probably don't have the time or the resources to deliver a broadcast-quality virtual presentation. But you absolutely can organize your virtual presentation more effectively. You can bring a higher level of enthusiasm to your presentations. You actually have more opportunities to get your audience involved in your presentation than the professionals do, and you have online tools available to you that are similar to those used by the pros.

Watch the evening news or your favorite talk show. Note the flow of the broadcast. Use the Sequencing Chart located at the end of this book to write down what happens during the broadcast.

You may find this exercise difficult because there are so many transitions, it is hard to note them all. However, this is an excellent exercise to get a feel for the pace and efficiency of a television or radio broadcast.

Use the Sequencing Chart as you participate in your next online meeting or virtual presentation.

Use it to organize your next virtual presentation. It will force you to prepare a detailed outline of your presentation.

FIVE NEWSCAST TECHNIQUES YOU CAN USE

The rest of this chapter explores five features of a radio or television newscast that are designed to grab and hold the attention of the viewing or listening audience. Stations are relentless in their pursuit of mastering these features so that their newscast is the one you choose to tune into day after day after day.

#1 Organization and sequencing

The **sequencing** of stories, guests, commercials, features, audio and video clips, graphics, music and interviews must fit together seamlessly. Topics, transitions, technology, talent and timing are meticulously planned. Planning is essential if success is to be achieved.

In broadcasting, they use what is referred to as a *rundown*. This is a detailed outline of the precise flow and timing of the broadcast. Precise sequencing is important for a local newscast, for example, because the program will cover local, regional and national news, weather and sports and typically a human-interest, humorous or entertaining story all in about 23 minutes (30 minutes minus commercial time). This cannot be accomplished without being well organized.

Newscasts are divided into **blocks or segments**. Each block covers a specific topic or story. The length of each block is determined by the importance of the topic and how long it will take to tell the story.

The producer or executive producer of the newscast will often select the reporter who will cover the story. If a reporter has personal experience with the topic, a solid understanding of the topic and an emotional connection with the topic, then it will be a more interesting and enlightening story for the audience. If a reporter finds a topic interesting, it is easier for her to make the story interesting to the audience. Keep that in mind the next time you host a virtual meeting and you are determining who is the best choice to lead a discussion on a specific topic.

A newscast is **a series of presentations**, just as a virtual meeting is a series of presentations. Each has a defined amount of time, a certain amount of information that needs to be covered and access to tools that can add impact to its delivery.

A rule of thumb when sequencing a newscast is, **"Most interesting first."** This is why most local newscasts begin with the sentence, "Good evening, our top story tonight . . ." Breaking news trumps all other news because of its lure of mystery and uncertainty. If it's breaking news, we expect to hear something we haven't heard before.

As you prepare your virtual presentations, answer five choice and timing questions:

1) What topics must I cover during this presentation or meeting?

2) How should I arrange the topics considering "Most interesting first?"

3) How deep do I need to go with each topic?

4) How much time, if any, should I devote to discussion or Q&A?

5) How much information can I realistically cover in the allotted time?

We will touch on these questions when we discuss planning and sequencing in chapter 4 ("Take Command of Your Message").

#2 Efficient use of time

Newscasts are highly organized, with efficiency being a top priority. Notice that none of the anchors or reporters ever appears rushed.

Anchors and reporters remain calm and professional at all times. Even *The Weather Channel* reporters, who are leaning into gale force winds and being pelted by raindrops traveling horizontally at 90 miles per hour, appear to have everything under control.

They are able to remain calm because they know how much time is allotted to the segment and they don't try to deliver more information than the allotted time can accommodate. They don't try to compress 60 minutes of information into a 30-minute show.

Efficiency is a must when you have 23 minutes to cover local, regional and national news, sports, weather, traffic and a special-interest story or two. There is no time to waste. There can be no downtime. You cannot get bogged down, for any reason.

The efficiency of the newscast even extends to the use of verbal graffiti (for example, "um," "uh," "you know," "I mean," or "like"). You rarely hear "um" and "uh" in a newscast. In the previously mentioned *NBC Nightly News* opening, Brian Williams did not begin by saying, "Um, good evening, uh, while uh few people were, you know, willing to, you know, say it like out loud, um . . ." Time is too precious. Every word counts. The use of verbal graffiti reflects a level of unpreparedness that is not acceptable. About the only time you will hear verbal graffiti during a newscast is when the anchors or reporters are speaking extemporaneously or responding to questions they were not prepared to answer, or when someone *on the street* is being interviewed.

#3 Roles

Each person in a newscast is assigned a role. Each role has a defined purpose. To be successful, each role needs to be performed with the highest level of professionalism.

Newscast roles can include anchor (news, sports, weather), reporter (in studio or remote), experts in a particular field (health, fitness, politics, community affairs), guests and commentators. In most markets a single newscast will involve eight to ten anchors and reporters.

In a talk show format, the talent can include a host, a cohost, guests, panelists, reporters, members of the production team, audience members and even musicians (Jay Leno and Kevin Eubanks; David Letterman and Paul Shaffer; and Ellen DeGeneres and Tony Okungbowa) who are involved with some aspect of the show.

A live audience will make the show more engaging to the viewing or listening audience. Hearing others laugh, clap and respond encourages viewers and listeners to get involved.

Behind the scenes are some of the most important roles in a broadcast. Television, for example, has directors, producers, writers, a camera crew, lighting and sound specialists, makeup artists and a host of other people who assist in the production and delivery of the show.

If we were to transfer the roles from television to our virtual presentations, the most important would be that of the producer. In a broadcast, the producer owns the show. The producer is responsible for making sure that what is supposed to happen, happens. When possible, assign someone the role of producer for your virtual presentation. Be sure to clearly define what your producer's responsibilities are—from getting everyone connected, to making sure the appropriate software and drivers are being used, to monitoring incoming questions, to conducting polls and surveys and any other production-related items.

Being the producer requires a commitment of time. The producer can assign some of the work to other participants. You might even assign a pre-presentation producer to handle many of the setup details, and a presentation producer to help during the live delivery of the virtual presentation.

In chapter 7 ("Don't Fly Solo") we will describe the roles in greater detail. The goal is to assign roles to make the organization and delivery of your virtual presentation as professional as possible.

#4 Transitions

The handoffs used by the professionals are smooth and efficient. There are no lingering or sluggish transitions. At least, not on purpose.

> Effective transitions eliminate awkward moments.

Listen to how the anchors and reporters transition into and out of segments. What phrases do they use to move from person to person or topic to topic? You can use most, if not all, of the transitions that they use in broadcasting when your presentation or meeting involves more than one presenter.

Simple is better when using transitions. In the last sentence of your presentation, use the name of the person you are transitioning to. This gives the next person a heads-up that you are completing your presentation, report or segment. Stating the next presenter's name is the most often used transition in broadcasting.

"Marty, we'll keep an eye on that, thanks."

"Back to you, Kaitlyn."

"It's the most snow we've had in 75 years. Frank."

"And Amy, this will not move forward until a decision is made."

We will cover transitions in greater detail in chapter 12 ("Create Seamless Transitions").

#5 Tools

Radio and television use all available tools to grab and maintain your interest and attention. Radio obviously has fewer tools because of a lack of visual contact with the audience.

You can use all of these tools to your advantage. Keep in mind, however, that the people on the screen or behind the microphone in broadcast-quality productions rarely control the audio and video portions of the broadcast. Some longtime radio hosts control their own board, but most have specialists do it for them. This is another potential job for the producer you recruit to help with your presentation.

Television Tools

- Video and video editing
- Photos
- Audio
- Slides
- Live or recorded talent
- Graphics—static or animated
- Interactive computer screens, whiteboards, and green screen technology
- Conversations, interviews and commentary
- Sounds, sound bites and sound effects
- Music

- Staging, backgrounds, sets, varied locations

Radio Tools

- Voice
- Audio
- Music
- Live or recorded talent
- Conversations, interviews and commentary
- Sounds, sound bites and sound effects
- Callers

Remember, the tools you use are only effective if they are used properly. Before your next virtual presentation, consider the following:

1) What tools are available for my virtual presentation?
2) Can I manage the tools alone, or do I need assistance?
3) What tools can be prepared in advance?
4) What tools can I use *in the moment*?
5) What tools will create the greatest impact?

SUCCESS COMES IN MANY FORMATS

Here are several radio and television programs that you can monitor in order to experience a wide array of delivery methods and techniques. Some of these programs use all of the latest and greatest technology while others are no-frills talk shows. The beauty of examining an array of delivery methods is that you will see that success does not require you to fit a specific mold. There are many formats that have proven successful. You might favor one format over another, or you might find that a combination of delivery methods leads to your desired results.

Television

The Tavis Smiley Show (PBS)

The Suze Orman Show (CNBC)

The Situation Room with Wolf Blitzer (CNN)

Live! With Regis and Kelly

British Broadcasting Corporation News (BBC)

Radio

Mike and Mike in the Morning (ESPN Radio)

Howard Stern (Sirius XM)

The Wall Street Journal Report

Wait, Wait . . . Don't Tell Me! (National Public Radio)

A Prairie Home Companion (American Public Media)

Search the web. Most corporate websites provide webcasts, podcasts and webinars. You will observe a variety of good and not-so-good techniques as you peruse these presentations.

As you read this book, focus on the techniques that best fit your personality style, your corporate culture, the technical capabilities available and most importantly, your audience.

 Just because people in your organization have always done it a certain way doesn't mean that there isn't a better way.

Be open to new techniques and modify them to your advantage. The safest place to practice using a new technique or technology is in a setting where you have nothing to lose. It is generally safer, and smarter, to try a new approach during a meeting with people you interact with on a regular basis. This assumes that you have practiced it several times prior to your *live* performance. You do not want your first live attempt at using a new technique or technology to occur during a meeting with your board of directors, a client or a prospect.

Build on your success. If a certain approach or delivery technique works, then keep using it. If a technique is clumsy or distracting, stop using it and practice it until it becomes natural and easy to execute.

CHAPTER 3
THE NUMBER ONE REASON VIRTUAL PRESENTATIONS FAIL

WHEN VIRTUAL PRESENTATIONS FAIL, people are quick to blame the technology and the remote aspects of these presentations. Participants are spread out in various locations and in multiple time zones. They are trying to get connected to the meeting, stay connected and figure out what buttons to push. Some of the participants and meeting leaders may be unfamiliar with or intimidated by the technology. Others may not be comfortable using the available tools.

However, when things go wrong, we can't just blame the technology. The technology is simply the vehicle for transporting the message to the audience. The number one reason virtual presentations fail is from a lack of planning.

An excellent example of how crucial it is to plan for and anticipate high-tech glitches occurred in June 2010, when Apple CEO Steve Jobs experienced a technology meltdown during his worldwide introduction of the iPhone 4. For Jobs, renowned for his well-orchestrated presentations and shock-and-awe product demos, the meltdown was brought on by an overloaded Wi-Fi network. Too many people in the audience were using the same wireless channel, and consequently, he was unable to access the Internet and complete the demo. Just a month earlier, a Google demonstration of its Internet television technology had been interrupted by a similar problem with an overloaded wireless network.

It used to be safe for companies to isolate a wireless channel that only they could access during product demonstrations. Today's technology, however, allows anyone with the right equipment to access any channel on the spectrum and create a hotspot. Jobs said that there were more than five hundred hotspots emanating from the audience.

I would bet that everyone reading this book has experienced the loss of connectivity or the incredibly slow processing time that results from being on an overloaded wireless network. Would you be willing to risk your worldwide product introduction on that wireless network? And would you take that risk without having a backup plan?

One commonsense backup plan is to produce a prerecorded demo. If all else fails, play the prerecorded video and let your presenter or presenters provide live commentary. After all, your objective is to have people *see* the improved features and capabilities of your new product.

Meltdowns are going to happen no matter how much you prepare and no matter who you are. With attention to detail in the planning phase, and applying lessons learned the hard way by other corporations, you can rise above a meltdown that happens on your watch.

POOR PLANNING LEADS TO POOR EXECUTION

As the saying goes, "If you fail to plan, plan to fail." Everything starts with planning. Without a well-designed plan, the execution phase becomes much more difficult. The effort you put into the planning phase of a virtual presentation will impact all aspects of the presentation.

Virtual presentations demand significant attention to detail in the planning phase. Before the presentation, you have to determine many more action items than you would for a typical in-person presentation. During the virtual presentation, you need to coordinate and implement all of these action items to ensure that the presentation runs smoothly and the desired actions are accomplished.

If you are able to skip the planning phase and *wing* your presentations—and you do it exceptionally well—then you are an anomaly. Few people are capable of delivering a strong presentation without preparing for it.

Occasionally I work with individuals who say, "I'm better off-the-cuff." I've yet to see anyone who is actually better *off-the-cuff* than they are after planning and practicing. A contemporary of former British Prime Minister Sir Winston Churchill once said, "Winston Churchill wasted some of the best years of his life preparing for his impromptu speeches."

Lack of planning leads to

- Presentations that are not necessary.
- Presentations that start and end late.
- Technology failures.
- Participants who have the wrong connection instructions or times.
- Confusion about the purpose of the presentation.

- Presentations that drift, get bogged down, or are difficult to follow.
- Off-topic questions, conversations and sidebars.
- Content that is irrelevant for some or all of the attendees.
- The wrong people attending.
- Participants having no part in the presentation.
- Lack of appropriate follow-up.

Planning involves more than just knowing what you want to say.

The negative results in the previous list don't have to occur. The power to prevent presentation failure lies in the hands of the presenter. All but a few of the reasons for failure are controllable if you have a process for organizing the presentation. If you have a plan in place, even the things you can't control, such as technology breakdowns, will not severely impact your presentation.

Over the last 10 years I have asked workshop participants to complete the following two sentences. You should complete these sentences as well.

In regard to presenting

1) I feel best when _____

_____

_____

2) I feel the worst when _____

_____

_____

The overwhelming majority of completed sentences for #1 have to do with preparation.

Examples: "I feel best when . . .

- I'm comfortable with the topic."
- I have clearly defined the goals of the presentation."
- I have time to prepare."
- I am able to stay on message."
- I understand the objectives of the meeting."

Other *feeling best* responses include issues such as knowing the audience members, presenting to an in-person audience, presenting to a small group, responding to questions and being able to interact with the audience.

Now let's move to sentence #2, "I feel the worst when

_____."

Again, the majority of responses related to preparation, or lack thereof.

Examples: "I feel worst when . . .

- I was unclear about the presentation goals."
- I don't know what outcomes are expected."
- I didn't have enough time to prepare."
- I can't stay focused."
- I get sidetracked and lose my direction."

Other *feeling worst* responses include not having rapport with the audience, the presentation being recorded, starting the presentation, not feeling like an expert on the topic, not being able to see or hear the audience and presenting to larger groups.

IF YOU WANT YOUR VIRTUAL PRESENTATION TO SUCCEED, DON'T LEAVE THE PREPARATION TO CHANCE

"Destiny is not a matter of chance, it is a matter of choice."
—William Jennings Bryant

Remember—the success or failure of a virtual presentation has to do with the planning you do before delivering the message. If you leave the destiny of your virtual presentation to chance, you are rolling the dice as to whether you succeed or fail.

The definitions of *fail* according to www.dictionary.com are

1) to fall short of success or achievement in something expected, attempted, desired or approved.

2) to receive less than a passing grade or mark in an examination, class, or course of study.

3) to be or become deficient or lacking; be insufficient or absent; fall short.

Think again about some of the virtual presentations you have attended, and then reread the definitions of fail. Did the presentations fall short of achieving something expected, attempted or desired? Were any expectations established to begin with? Did these virtual presentations receive a less-than-passing grade or evaluation? Were these presentations deficient or lacking? Did they fall short?

 Practice will improve your confidence, content, delivery and timing.

Blog entry from Carol in Cleveland, Ohio

I was invited to join a virtual meeting in which eight of the participants were together in a conference room in downtown Cleveland. Four people, including me, were participating remotely. The purpose of the meeting was to review a marketing plan. I thought my part in the meeting was to share my thoughts regarding the plan, but no one directly defined my role.

As I evaluate the experience, here are some of my thoughts:

- No one sent me an agenda prior to the meeting, so I didn't know the meeting schedule, topics or objectives. All I knew was the starting time and the number to connect to the meeting.
- The speakerphone in the conference room was not centrally located. It was exceedingly hard to hear what people in the conference room were saying unless they were sitting directly in front of the speakerphone.
- When humorous comments were made during the presentation, I could only hear mumbled words followed by a burst of laughter. I felt a bit left out.
- Participants failed to identify themselves when making a comment, so I was in the dark as to who was talking and what role that person was playing in the project.
- I could hear cell phones ringing and people answering them.
- People were jumping in and out of the meeting without notice. At one point, a question asked to a remote participant was followed by a long awkward silence because the person who had been asked the question had left the meeting, without letting anyone know.

- I could hear a keyboard being tapped on throughout the entire meeting. It was irritating. 💬

Was this virtual presentation a success or a failure? From Carol's vantage point, it was a failure. It was like listening to an AM radio station while sitting under electric power lines. She could hear a portion of what was being said but not enough to follow the flow of information and the concepts being discussed. Carol commented that she was quick to disconnect at the end of the meeting.

Was the meeting a success for the people in the conference room? Carol never knew. She didn't receive any follow-up information.

Some of the blame for Carol's bad experience falls directly on her shoulders. She could have requested a copy of the meeting agenda. She could have talked with someone involved in the planning of the meeting about the role she would assume. During the meeting, she could have informed the meeting leader that she could not hear much of what was being said. But she was unfamiliar with the group and, therefore, a bit shy about making those requests.

On the other hand, if the leader of the meeting had planned more diligently, the negative aspects of the meeting would not have occurred. The entire list of problems is easily correctable.

- Send an agenda to all participants prior to the presentation. Include the meeting objectives, the topics to be discussed, a rundown listing the timing of the segments, the names and titles of all of the participants and the information needed to connect to the meeting.
- Situate the speakerphone so that everyone can be heard. Remind the in-person participants to speak clearly and loudly enough to be heard and understood.
- If there is any chance that something said was not heard by everyone, repeat what had been said.

- The first time someone makes a comment, that person should state his name, his title and his role in the project. Thereafter, he should state his name at the beginning of any additional comments.

- The pre-meeting material should set the ground rules that include the banning of cell phones, emailing, texting or activities that can distract the attendees or the presenters.

- Establish a signal that lets everyone know when someone removes herself from the meeting and when she returns.

- If typing on a keyboard is necessary, make sure the keyboard is not located next to the speakerphone.

The negative aspects of Carol's meeting all had to do with planning. Most are commonsense errors or issues that resulted because the leader didn't take the time to think about the basic communication needs of the participants.

To become a more confident and impactful virtual presenter, make preparation your top priority. Thorough planning will lead to more consistent results. By adopting a more systematic approach to organizing and delivering your virtual presentations, you will exceed participant expectations every time, and your audiences will come to expect the best whenever you are leading a presentation.

KEEP IT RELEVANT

Your virtual presentation must be relevant, or it will be ignored.

EVERYTHING IN YOUR VIRTUAL PRESENTATION must be of interest to the audience. Keeping everything relevant is the only chance you have to capture and keep their attention. The distractions are bountiful.

Throughout the entire process of planning, selecting the topics, delivering your message and following up with your participants, stay focused on keeping every piece of information relevant. If it's not relevant, don't include it.

CHAPTER 4
TAKE COMMAND OF YOUR MESSAGE

AS YOU ORGANIZE YOUR VIRTUAL PRESENTATION, keep in mind that your message is your personal brand. It represents who you are. It represents your level of experience. It is a reflection of your intellect and your ability to articulate your thoughts. It tells others a lot about how you think and how you organize. With so much riding on your message, it is worth taking the time to organize it in a systematic, thorough and consistent manner.

DEFINE YOUR PURPOSE AND FRAME YOUR PRESENTATION

Because the level of planning for a virtual presentation requires more organization and detail than an in-person presentation does, it is critical that you begin by defining the purpose of your presentation.

If you can't clearly define the purpose of your presentation, don't schedule it.

It is helpful to be able to frame the first 60–90 seconds of your presentation by leading your audience through the

- Purpose (or goal/mission/objective) of the presentation.
- Key take-away points.
- Agenda.
- Situation as you understand it.
- End result, consequences, ramifications or benefits of action or inaction.

The only way to state these five components in 90 seconds or less is to be hyperefficient with your wording. If the first 60–90 seconds of your presentation are clear and concise, you will appear more organized to your audience.

In the first 60–90 seconds,

- State the **purpose (or goal/mission/objective)** of the meeting. What is it that you want to accomplish in the time you are with your audience? For example, say: "The purpose of the meeting today is to resolve any pending issues related to the Acme account."
- Tell the audience the **key take-away points.** This will help focus their attention on the information that is at the heart of your message. For example, say: "I need you to keep three key points in mind during this presentation: Point number one . . ."

- Briefly, state the **agenda**. The agenda tells your audience what you plan to cover. This should be a high-level, concise snapshot of what you will cover in the body of your presentation. You do not need to list every item. Save the details for the presentation itself.

You should be able to state the agenda in 30 seconds or less. For example, say: "The agenda for this presentation will include the following: First, Ryan will review our Q4 results. Next, Robin will provide a report on the City of Chicago proposal. And finally, Neil will facilitate a discussion designed to formulate three strategies for making our virtual client meetings more productive."

Additional examples: "I plan to update you this morning on two possible outcomes in the Acme case." Or, "My agenda is to share three strategies that will allow us to stay close to our customers."

- Outline the **situation** as you understand it. What position(s) has been established? What issues are at play? For example, say: "The situation, as we understand it, is that you are experiencing slow connect times with your current provider." Or, "The primary issues that you have brought to our attention relate to . . ."

- Be able to verbalize the **end result, consequences, ramifications or benefits** that are occurring or will occur because of the situation. For example, say: "As a result of not having enough product in the warehouse, we are losing orders." Or, "The end result is that our customer service numbers have risen in the last 90 days."

Once you have determined the most concise way to state the components of your opening, you can put them together, in any order, to create your 60- to 90-second opening statement. For example:

The **objective** of today's meeting is to identify new strategies that will add value for our customers and, at the same time, generate additional sales going forward.

The **situation** is that our customers have fewer resources for upgrading their existing systems. They are facing more restrictions on the funding they can use to replace those systems.

As a result, our customers are losing confidence in our ability to provide solutions. That, in turn, has caused our sales to plummet over the last 12 months.

My **agenda** this morning is threefold: First, I will review our sales performance over the last 12 months. Second, Regan is going to tell us how she was able to help XYZ Company secure the funding to purchase our newest technology. And finally, Nolan will facilitate a brainstorming session in which we will identify at least three new strategies to help our customers secure the funding they need to purchase new systems and stay competitive.

If you **take one point away** from this presentation, I want you to remember this: We must add value by finding ways to help our customers fund the new systems. If we do that, our sales results will recover rapidly.

Let's start with our performance over the last 12 months.

One other component to include in your presentation is to define the **next steps**. Give clear direction and timing for the next steps to be accomplished. Be sure to indicate by whom and by when the steps need to be completed. If the next steps are known at the beginning of the meeting, you can include them in your opening statement. However, if they will be determined throughout the presentation, they can serve as a way to end your presentation with an action plan for the participants. For example, say:

"Therefore our next step is to contact Jeanne and set up an appointment to finalize the contract by Friday the 2nd."

"Before we wrap up this meeting, I'd like Tom, Julia, Paul and Erin to tell me your next steps, as well as the timing and date by which you will have completed those steps."

"The next steps are (1) to identify the three strategies to help our customers secure funding and (2) develop our individual business plans around those strategies. Your plans should be completed and emailed to me by Wednesday, the 22nd."

Those of you who have read my book *The Exceptional Presenter* will notice that you can use a structure to frame your virtual presentations similar to the one you use to frame your face-to-face presentations. This structure is also effective when you are preparing for question-and-answer sessions and for media interactions and when you are preparing to be interviewed.

Use this format to frame each topic in your virtual presentation so each topic can stand alone, if needed.

SELECT AND SEQUENCE YOUR TOPICS

In order to grab the attention of your audience, begin your presentation with your most interesting topic. If you capture their attention at the start of your presentation, you have a good chance of maintaining it throughout the presentation.

The most interesting topic is not always your core message, but it should always be 100 percent relevant to the audience. It can include a variety of information. Perhaps one of your competitors is in play to be taken over. Or your business unit is coming out with a revamped compensation package that will impact everyone in the meeting. Or an event has taken place that could possibly allow new markets to open up for your product or service.

Sequence the topics in the order you feel will sustain a high level of interest on the part of your participants. Align the topics in a way that will fulfill the purpose of the meeting and keep your participants alert, interested and informed.

Refrain from determining how much time to spend on each topic until you have answered these three important questions:

1) What topics need to be addressed?

2) What topics will help to accomplish the purpose of the presentation?

3) What level of detail is needed to cover each topic?

Answer these three questions to ensure that your topics are relevant and are not just wedged into your presentation to fill time.

Blog entry from Bill in Cincinnati, Ohio

I received a call from one of our senior partners. He reminded me that our quarterly, 2-day conference was 2 weeks away. He said that I should come up with a presentation that we could insert into the agenda, because right now we only have enough topics for a 1-day conference. My immediate response was, 'Why not just make it a 1-day conference?' I assume we proceeded to have the 2-day conference because the dates were already scheduled. Day one was time well spent. The energy and participation levels were high. We accomplished a great deal. Day two? Not so good. We filled time with slides, talk and not-so-important information. Very little was accomplished. Considering who was in the audience and what they charge per hour, day two was an expensive waste of time. 💬

BREAK THE PRESENTATION INTO SEGMENTS

Make your virtual presentations more interesting and more efficient by breaking them into segments. Just as newscasts are a sequence of short stories, the topics in your virtual presentations should be divided into a sequence of fast-paced, well-connected segments. Breaking a topic into segments allows you to change the pace, tempo or direction of the presentation on a continuous basis. It enables you to keep refocusing the attention of the audience to your material and prevents the audience from being overexposed to a single topic. It also helps prevent the occurrence of long-winded and uninterrupted monologues.

You don't need to provide your audience with every available detail about a specific topic. Tell them what they need to know and move on. You can give them more detail in the follow-up material if you determine that they need to know more about the topic or if they request additional information.

How long should each segment last? That depends on the topic and on the material being covered. As a general rule, shorter is better. Try to restrict each segment to less than 5 minutes. Remember that a single topic can be composed of several segments.

For Example:

Topic: Review progress of XYZ Company pursuit team

Segment	Who	Time
Overview of XYZ status	Dave	2 minutes
Progress report	Kathy	3 minutes
Timeline for proposal	Amy	30 seconds
Open discussion of options	ALL	5 minutes

ESTABLISH THE FINAL AGENDA, TIMING AND FLOW

You have defined your purpose and framed your presentation. You have selected the topics and determined the sequencing of those topics. You have thought about how to break the topics into manageable and digestible segments. At this point, you can determine time allocations for each topic. Don't establish the time parameters of the meeting and then find topics to fill the time.

Fill out a copy of the Sequencing Chart located at the end of this book. Armed with a completed chart that includes the list of topics, segments, people responsible and time allotted, you can now establish the agenda, timing and flow for the entire presentation. By laying out this information, you will be able to see how much information you need to cover during your presentation. This is your reality check to see if it is possible and practical to cover all of the information in a single presentation.

Part of determining the flow is deciding what you want your audience to see and hear during the presentation. Is it necessary for the participants to see the presenters? If so, whose image do you want visible on the screen during the various topics and segments? Will there be a slide deck displayed during the presentation? Are you going to show video clips? Will you be accessing the Internet? What is the best way to get feedback from the participants? Do you need to hear the participants, or can they participate via text, email, IM or chat?

Deciding what will be on the screen, and when it will be visible, is an important step in the process that will help determine the most effective means of connecting with the participants. Use the Sequencing Chart from the time you begin thinking about the structure of your presentation. The information on your Sequencing Chart will most likely change several times before you finalize the sequence and flow of the presentation.

DETERMINE WHO SHOULD PARTICIPATE

The best time to determine who should attend the presentation is after you have decided what information you plan to cover. Knowing what information will be covered helps you determine the relevance of the information to the people you want to invite. If Bob has no interest in or doesn't need to know about the topics being covered, why would you want to invite Bob? It will be a waste of Bob's time.

At this point you can also finalize your decision as to who will present each of the topics. (See chapter 7, "Don't Fly Solo," for a description of roles.) Determining what transitions to use during the presentation (person to person and topic to topic) will take place once you start practicing the presentation.

CHOOSE THE TECHNOLOGY

Now it's time to determine the best meeting method for your virtual presentation. There are a multitude of options available to deliver your message. Some will be outdated by the time this book reaches your hands. The technology is continually changing and morphing into new and hybrid technologies.

Whatever technology you choose, don't let it intimidate you. Keep it simple. The thought of delivering a presentation can be intimidating by itself. Throw in the technology factor, and soon your nerves start telling you to cancel the presentation.

When deciding which technology to use, ask yourself these important questions:

1) What is at stake with this presentation? What is at risk?

    High stakes example: If you are trying to convert a prospect into a customer and you can't meet face-to-face, select the most intimate setting possible. Select the setting in which you can see your audience and they can see you. The most intimate virtual options tend to be the high-end options such as telepresence.

Low stakes example: If you are meeting with your team where the participants are familiar with each other and the issues, then your choice is less critical.

2) Which technology will allow you to deliver your material with the greatest impact?

Determine what you need to show, explain or display during your presentation. Then choose the technology that provides the best set of tools for your material.

3) Which technology will create the most comfortable environment for you and your audience?

Is it important for your audience to see you? What purpose will it serve for your face to be on the screen?

You may not be comfortable with your image on screen. It may make you feel self-conscious and distract you or make you less effective in delivering your message. On the other hand, consider whether your objective is to be comfortable or to persuade the audience. If your message will be better delivered with your image on screen, then get over the fear, practice your on-screen delivery and choose a technology that allows your image to be visible to your audience.

4) Do you need to see your audience members? Which audience members need to be visible to you?

Consider if and why audience members need to be on the screen. Perhaps it will help you to make sure they are listening to you and not multitasking. You will be able to see their reactions to the information you are presenting. Or maybe you want to get a better overall impression of how they feel via their body language, facial expressions, gestures and voice.

5) Are they going to be comfortable knowing that their image is on the screen?

Think about whether being visible on the screen will prompt your audience to be more involved or if it will temper their enthusiasm and cause them to clam up. Younger people seem to be less timid about being on the screen, perhaps because they have grown up in a technology-driven world where having their image on a computer or smart phone screen is an everyday occurrence.

During most of my presentation skills training sessions, I video record the participants. I have worked with very few participants who actually enjoy seeing themselves on the screen. They get used to it the more video recording we do. I suggest that your comfort level with being on screen will improve with each video-based virtual presentation that you conduct. The more you do it, the more comfortable you will become with your image being on the screen.

6) How comfortable is your audience with the technology? How will their interaction with the technology impact their participation?

If the audience is uncomfortable with the technology but is forced to use it to participate, their overall experience will be less than exceptional. If they are comfortable with the technology, they are more likely to stay engaged and participate. If their involvement is important but the technology intimidates them, then you have to make a concerted effort to educate them as to how to use it. Make sure they understand that their participation is important. Call on your tech support person to help participants with the technology both prior to the presentation and as the technology is being applied during the presentation.

When choosing the technology, consider these factors as well:

- Which will allow the greatest ease of preparation for everyone involved?
- Which will allow the participants to connect to the presentation with the least hassle?
- Which will be the easiest technology for the presenters and the participants to operate and manage during the presentation?

Let's now focus on the major technologies available for virtual presentations.

Telepresence is the high-end, state-of-the art option that was developed to create a completely immersive experience. The configuration of the room replicates a conference room setting. Telepresence uses multiple speakers to reproduce audio in all directions, which makes it sound as if all participants are in the same room. The video screens are ultra-high-definition, and the images of the participants are life-size. Everyone can observe body language, movement, facial expressions and eye contact as if they were in the same room. It is easy for participants to connect to the meeting. Desktops can be shared.

If you have the opportunity to present your information using telepresence, do it! If you can't be there face-to-face in the same room as the people you are meeting with, it's the next best thing. Everything about the room is designed to feel as if you are all in the same room. The lighting, the chairs, the continuous conference table that extends into the other group's space and the special audio features are consistent in all locations. Telepresence was designed to eliminate the feeling that technology is involved.

The higher the stakes of your presentation, the more important it is for the setting to look and feel as face-to-face as possible. For high stakes presentations when you can't be there, telepresence is a smart choice.

But not everyone has the option for telepresence meetings. Using these rooms is more costly than most other virtual options are. The number of available telepresence rooms is somewhat limited, so you might have to work around other people's schedules. However, more and more companies are installing telepresence and videoconference rooms. Hotels and conference centers are adding high-end virtual presentation capability to their meeting rooms in order to adapt to the changing travel and budget parameters many of their customers face.

Webcast. If your message will be more impactful through the use of video in addition to audio, a webcast is another option for your virtual presentation. Webcasts allow for primarily one-way communication of voice, video, audio and visuals. If you select the webcast format, your interaction with the audience is somewhat limited. You can create participation that typically involves a question-and-answer session conducted by a moderator who can control the flow of information. It is more difficult to judge the interest level of your audience with a webcast. Your ability to have the audience actively participate is more restricted than with some of the other virtual options.

Web conferencing allows you to have anyone, anywhere, share anything, in real time. Web conferencing allows multiple participants in multiple locations to communicate interactively. It allows for the sharing of any desktop as well as the ability to change the leadership role during the presentation. It provides an almost limitless range of virtual tools to be utilized during your presentation. Web conferencing offers the use of interactive features, such as the ability to draw, use graphics, chat, vote and poll. You have the ability to show video clips and to stream video from the Internet and other sources. During web conferences, you can display the faces of both the leaders and the participants. Webinars fall under the blanket of web conferencing.

Conference calls provide a tried-and-true means of

communicating with multiple participants. They are one of the simplest choices for virtual presentations. There is no visual effect with conference calls, but you can create a visual element to the presentation. By emailing your presentation material to the participants, you can create a webinar feel to your call. You don't have control of what is being seen or when it is being seen, but you can provide the audience with visual support via PowerPoint or Keynote slides in order to add a visual component.

A link page can be added to any of the above-mentioned virtual categories. A linkinar occurs when you attach links to a document, email the document to the participants and then have them click the links as you direct them during the presentation. You can link to just about anything on the web. It's as easy as saying to the participants: "Now please click on link number one. What you see is the . . ."

Sending a link document is one way to beef up your conference call or phone call. Creating a link document is quick, easy and inexpensive.

Peer-to-peer applications enable people who have accounts on the same system to have video-based communication and have the ability to share their desktops. Skype and Oovoo are two examples of peer-to-peer applications. Most allow multiple faces from multiple locations to be on the screen at the same time (the Hollywood Squares or Brady Bunch effect). This is a quick and easy way to connect.

Ultimately, your choice of technology should be driven by what is most compatible with your personal communication style, your message and what will best serve your audience. If you and your audience are comfortable, the experience will be more conducive to open and productive conversation and to the sharing of information and ideas. Find the technology that you are comfortable with, or get used to the one that your company provides.

The virtual presentation industry is moving toward an *any to any* scenario. The industry vision is that any virtual presentation

technology will be able to connect with any other virtual presentation technology. It is already possible for participants to join the
meeting from any number of sources. For example, you can now
join a telepresence meeting via a computer or a smart phone.

The success of your virtual presentation will have more to do
with your preparation and delivery than with the technology you
choose. But your comfort level with the technology will affect the
flow of information and the ease with which you involve the audience. Keep it simple and choose the technology that will best serve
your message.

If your goal is to deliver a presentation that captivates your audience and moves them to take action, then you must start by taking
command of your message.

VIRTUAL PREP SHEET

NAME: TIME:
MEETING NAME: DATE:

"The purpose (or objective/mission/goal) of my presentation today is to . . .

_____

_____."

"If you remember only one (two, three) point(s) from this presentation, remember this . . .

_____

_____

_____."

"The agenda for this presentation includes . . . (This must be brief, less than 30 seconds.)

_____

_____

_____."

"The situation is as follows" OR "We are positioned as follows . . .

_____

_____."

"The end result (consequence/ramification/benefit) is . . .

_____

_____."

"The next step(s) is to . . .

_____

_____."

End the presentation with a purpose statement: "I'd like you to leave here remembering one important point . . .

_____

_____."

CONTENT

1) What topics will I cover and in what sequence, considering "Most important first"?

_____   _____   _____

2) How deep do I need to go with each topic?

3) How much time for discussion or Q&A?

4) What resources can I use to prepare?

DELIVERY

Method?

What tools are available?

Can I manage the tools alone, or do I need assistance?

      Who will fill the role of producer?

      Who will provide tech support?

Who else should be involved in the presentation? What role?

Name: Role: Assignment:

Name: Role: Assignment:

TO DO
- Complete the Sequencing Chart
- Get participant list, locations and local times
- Send a copy of the meeting agenda to all participants
- Send meeting expectations and info regarding anything they need to prepare or think about
-
-

FOLLOW-UP
- Who will be responsible for coordinating follow-up?
- Provide summary of presentation, support material, web links and contact information
- Send presentation evaluations
-
-

Copyright 2010 Timothy Koegel

SEQUENCING CHART Timing, Topics, Talent, Tools and Transitions

Name of presentation or meeting: _____

Technology: _____

Role: _____

Segment objectives: _____

_____

Topics to cover: _____

_____

Time	Topic	Talent (Who?) and Tools (What will be used?)	Transition Used

CHAPTER 5
HELP YOUR PARTICIPANTS PREPARE

EVERYONE'S TIME IS VALUABLE. Therefore, the individuals you have approached to participate in your meeting deserve every opportunity to succeed. As the meeting leader or host, you should provide enough direction and instruction so your attendees can efficiently organize their material and can participate enthusiastically.

ESTABLISH EXPECTATIONS AND RESPONSIBILITIES

All of the participants need to understand what will be expected of them and what they will be responsible for during the meeting. Every person involved in the virtual presentation has an important role to play. Whether your role is that of a non-presenting participant or of hosting the meeting, leading a segment, facilitating a discussion, providing tech support or helping to produce the presentation, you must own your role.

(One way to communicate these expectations and responsibilities is to send the participants an email message in advance of the meeting that covers the topics described in the rest of this chapter).

Own the role

In the book *The Exceptional Presenter: A Proven Formula to Open Up! and Own the Room,* the term "own the room" refers to an acting term describing someone who is so completely into character that he walks onto the stage with total confidence. He owns the room. As it relates to presenting, own the room means presenting with total confidence, maintaining the highest level of professionalism and holding oneself accountable for the success or failure of the presentation.

"Own" the role means that you are accountable for the success or failure of the part of the virtual presentation you have been charged to execute. It means doing whatever it takes to ensure that everyone attending stays engaged and understands your key points. If everyone involved in the meeting commits to owning his or her role and being accountable for the results, then it will be a productive meeting. The responsibilities of any role in a virtual presentation include planning, execution and follow-up.

Your assignment and preparation

The assignment of roles is designed to get more people involved, to bring your best resources and talent to the presentation and to make the presentation more interesting.

Each participant who has been assigned a role should receive a Virtual Prep Sheet, a Sequencing Chart and a Role Guidelines form. All three forms are located in the back of this book. We reviewed the Virtual Prep Sheet and Sequencing Chart in chapter 4 ("Take Command of Your Message"). A sample of a completed Role Guidelines form can be found at the end of this chapter. This form allows the meeting leader to provide specific instructions for and give direction to each presenter. All of these resources will help enable presenters and support personnel alike to prepare to execute their roles.

Every participant should receive a copy of the agenda. The purpose of the agenda is to provide the participants with a better sense of the overall meeting objectives. A list of available communication tools (for example, desktop sharing, surveys and chat) should be attached to the agenda.

Presenters must send their follow-up material to the meeting leader. The leader will provide the presenters with a date by which all follow-up material is due.

Each and every presenter should prepare as if his or her presentation is the most important segment of the meeting. All presenters should be resourceful, have fun and own their role.

How can non-presenting participants make the meeting a success? One word—PARTICIPATE

If you are not assigned a presentation during a meeting, your role is to participate. Participate is a verb. Synonyms include: contribute, partake, chip in, involve yourself, share, and play a part. Your responsibility is to do all of the above.

Be present. Be fully engaged. Listen. Think. Share your comments when appropriate. Be mindful of timing. Know when to comment, when to refrain from commenting and when to stop talking.

Use the available tools to communicate questions, comments, feelings and attitudes to the presenters. The presenters will be requesting that you respond to polls and surveys, as well as to provide feedback.

Give each presenter your undivided attention. If you are multitasking, your attention is divided, and you are not fully engaged.

Respect the presenters and the time they have invested in preparing for the meeting. As a general rule, don't do anything during this virtual presentation that you would not do if you were in the same room with the presenter. It is disrespectful to do things during a virtual meeting that would be considered inappropriate in an in-person meeting.

GET EVERYONE CONNECTED

To ensure that everyone is ready to start the meeting on time, provide the participants with specific instructions for signing on or logging in. Send out a meeting reminder that covers all of the pertinent details. What phone number should they call? What password should they use? How do they access the website or program to display the visuals? Do they need to download any software? If so, how do they access it?

Establish an expectation of punctuality. Suggest that everyone sign in 5 minutes before the start time. Let them know how to contact technical support if they have problems connecting. Delaying the meeting start time because participants are late signing in is a waste of everyone's time. Even more distracting is when people are still beeping in 5 minutes after the meeting has begun. Does the leader stop to acknowledge their arrival and to bring them up to speed? Does the person arriving late interrupt to apologize? Does the meeting continue in the hope that the late-arriving participants will figure out what is being presented? Punctuality on the part of the participants will eliminate many of the frustrations that are caused by late arrivals.

Everyone involved in the meeting should be connected before the meeting begins. An effective leader does everything possible to enable the participants to do so.

Helping your participants prepare for your virtual meetings will lead to a higher level of accomplishment and enjoyment of the meeting. It will also result in a lower level of stress and frustration among the role players prior to the meeting.

KEEP IT ENGAGING

Your virtual presentation must be engaging, or it will be forgotten.

YOU HAVE MADE A COMMITMENT to keep everything in your virtual presentation relevant. By doing so, you have already taken a major step toward the goal of keeping your presentation engaging.

Keeping your presentation engaging is your most difficult task. You can control the planning and structuring of your presentation. You can control the flow of the information to your audience. You can control what your audience sees and hears. What you can't control is your audience. You can't force your audience to pay attention. You can't control their surroundings or keep the audience from multitasking. And in many virtual presentations, you can't even see or hear what they are doing.

Therefore, keeping it engaging is critical if your virtual presentations are going to succeed. You must ramp up your level of enthusiasm and focus on being compelling throughout your entire presentation.

CHAPTER 6

MAKE YOUR PRESENTATION MORE INTERESTING THAN ANY OF THE DISTRACTIONS

FOR ANYONE PRESENTING INFORMATION VIRTUALLY, the greatest challenge lies in making the presentation more interesting than the distractions. Without a resolute commitment to achieving that objective, you will not achieve it.

Maintaining the attention of an in-person audience is challenging. When your audience is in far-off locations, you have to be relentless in your effort to get them involved and keep them engaged. The distractions are plentiful. Some are distractions you have not had to deal with during your face-to-face presentations. The barriers in virtual presentations are substantial.

By being vigilant about keeping every aspect of your presentation relevant, as discussed in the first segment of this book, you have already taken the first step to ensuring that every aspect of your virtual presentation will engage your audience. If everything your audience hears is relevant, the audience will pay attention, and you will have made significant progress toward ensuring that your message is retained.

Most of the questions I receive regarding virtual presentations do not involve the technology being used. Most often the questions are about how to create an in-person experience and how to overcome barriers that exist when presenting to remote audiences.

The following are fundamental concepts provided to help make sure that your audience stays engaged in your presentation. They involve a dynamic delivery, a commitment, your participant selection process, a singular focus and an awareness that attention is fleeting. Always keep these concepts in mind as you plan your virtual presentations.

MAKE IT HARD TO LOOK AWAY

I am always riveted to the television screen when I watch the downhill ski races during the Winter Olympics. Once a skier leaves the starting gate, I can't look away, for any reason. If anyone walks into the room and wants my attention, they immediately get the *talk-to-the-hand* pose and a rapid-fire series of "shushes."

Ever since Austrian downhill ski champion Franz Klammer won the gold medal at the Winter Olympics at Innsbruck, Austria, the downhill races have captivated my attention. Klammer's winning race was an all-out, push-it-beyond-the-limit, risk-everything quest to be the best downhiller in the world. Expectations were exceedingly high that Klammer would win the gold medal for the host country. During Klammer's winning effort, announcer

Bob Beattie exclaimed, "I've never seen so much pressure on one man in my entire life."

Every inch of the course was lined with rows of exceedingly enthusiastic Austrians. Klammer nearly wiped out several times during the race, and he was within a few feet of skiing into the crowd twice. Announcers Frank Gifford and Bob Beattie were wildly animated, shouting, "He's all over the course," "He's on the edge of disaster," "Look at him fly," "Franz Klammer can't be accused of anything but attacking" and "He almost went into the nets, but he's still going."

It had all the elements of a thriller movie—speed, daring, fear, risk, danger, suspense, anticipation and pressure. It was a remarkable demonstration of skill. It was one of the greatest performances in the history of sports. I recently watched the race again via YouTube and could not look away during the race. I was tense watching the video despite already knowing the outcome.

Distractions only distract when interest starts to wane.

A great deal of research has been conducted around the show *Sesame Street*, going all the way back to the show's inception. One of the interesting findings was that it is difficult to distract a child who is fully engrossed in a show. When the child begins to lose interest in what is on the screen, only then can the distractions grab the child's attention.

I suggest that what is true for a child watching *Sesame Street* is also true for an adult attending your virtual presentation. If a member of your audience is totally engrossed in your presentation, the distractions will not sidetrack him. It is when he begins to lose interest in your presentation that the distractions start shouting his name.

How can you make your virtual presentations riveting? How can you captivate your audience members to the point where they will assume the *talk-to-the-hand* position and shush any potential interruptions? By applying the techniques outlined in this book, you can make it much more difficult for your audience members to look away.

MAKE A COMMITMENT AND ASK FOR A COMMITMENT

At the beginning of your virtual presentation, tell your audience that you promise to be brief if they promise to give you their undivided attention.

For example, say:

Thank you for joining the meeting. Before we begin, I'd like to ask for a commitment from you, and in turn,

I will make a commitment to you. Give me your undivided attention for the next 25 minutes. In turn, I will give you three strategies that will help you generate additional opportunities with your existing clients.

Allow me to clarify one thing. The term 'undivided attention' means that you will focus your attention only on this presentation. Doing anything else (pause), anything else, is by definition multitasking. Multitasking is a violation of your commitment.

You can signify your commitment by sending me your initials via the chat feature right now. (Pause) Great, let's get started. For the remaining 24 minutes, I want you to focus on three key points . . .

This is a much more difficult commitment for people to make if the meeting is going to last for an extended period of time. If you keep the presentation succinct, you have a better chance of keeping the audience engaged. If you are stingy with your time during the planning phase, you will find ways to shorten the amount of time you need to conduct the presentation and fulfill your commitment.

MAKE SURE THE RIGHT PEOPLE ARE ATTENDING

Have you ever left a presentation, virtual or in person, thinking, "I have no idea why I was invited to that meeting." Most people answer that question, "Yes, I have, many times."

Blog entry from Sue in Charleston, South Carolina

I was invited to attend a presentation. I attended out of obligation. I had no interest in or connection to the topic. I saw no benefit, advantage or profit to be gained by attending. 💬

What are the odds that Sue will be an enthusiastic and active participant in the meeting? The answer is slim to none, unless something unexpectedly grabs her attention. To Sue, the time spent in a meeting that is irrelevant is time better spent accomplishing other tasks. Therefore, Sue is likely to use the time during the meeting to do other things—check and send email messages, organize her To Do list and text her coworkers about what a total waste of time the meeting is.

Virtual presentations have proven to be an effective and efficient way to present information and ideas. But just like face-to-face presentations, virtual presentations can be a big time waster when the wrong people are in attendance. If only half of the information is relevant to certain participants, let those participants exit the meeting once they have heard what they need to hear. Then continue the meeting with the remaining participants. Or schedule two start times that allow for certain attendees to be involved in part one of the meeting, certain attendees to be involved in part two of the meeting and certain attendees to be involved in both parts of the meeting.

Don't invite people to your presentation just to give them something to do. They already have more than enough to do. They can't afford to waste time on information that doesn't add value to their day.

Chapter 4 ("Take Command of Your Message") included a section entitled, "Determine who should participate." As you peruse the attendee list, answer this question, "Why is it important for this person to attend?" If you don't have a compelling answer to that question, don't invite that person.

MULTITASKING DOESN'T WORK, FOR YOU OR YOUR AUDIENCE

Multitasking has become a way of life in this digital age. Multitaskers are convinced that they are accomplishing more by multitasking. Remember the statistic stated earlier that 58 percent of the executives in the *Forbes Insights* survey see digital presentations as an opportunity to multitask and get other things done?

Let's see what the research from a Stanford University study tells us about multitasking. Stanford researchers Eyal Ophir, Clifford Nass and Anthony Wagner were curious as to why so many people these days are able to multitask when classical psychological textbooks tell us that it is psychologically impossible to process more than one string of information at a time. The researchers were hoping to find out what makes multitaskers special and what enables them to manage multiple streams of information simultaneously. "We kept looking for what they were better at," said Ophir.

The researchers were "absolutely shocked" by what they found. The research, released in August 2009, concluded that people who multitask are "lousy" at multitasking.

- People who multitask are constantly distracted by irrelevant information.

- People who multitask are less effective at storing and organizing information than people who are not multitasking.

- People who multitask are ineffective at switching from one thing to another. "They couldn't help thinking about the task they weren't doing," Ophir said. Multitasking slows down their processing time.

Professor Nass put it this way: "They seem to like being flooded with information. It's almost as if they prefer to scan the environment, just constantly scan and grab new information, rather than ponder what they have. We don't know if there are any advantages to that, but so far we haven't found any."

These research findings about multitasking are tremendously valuable as you plan and deliver your information. The findings imply that if an audience member is multitasking during your presentation,

1) She cannot, by definition, give you her undivided attention.

2) She is most likely not assimilating and storing the information that she sees or hears.

3) Her understanding of your message will be shallow because she is constantly scanning for more information rather than focusing solely on your material.

This information should motivate you to keep your audience singularly focused on your presentation. Start with the difficult challenge of persuading them to shut down all of their communication devices. In order to achieve a successful result, you have to be vigilant about getting everyone focused on only one string of information—yours.

> Of multitaskers, Stanford professor Clifford Nass says, "They're suckers for irrelevancy. Everything distracts them."

The Stanford research indirectly tells us that a multitasking presenter is a distracted presenter. Multitasking will affect your delivery. If you are monitoring incoming questions, conducting surveys and managing your slides while you are delivering the presentation, you are multitasking.

A Virginia Tech Transportation Institute study revealed that the risk of collision is 23 times greater when a driver is texting versus when a driver is not texting. Likewise, it seems obvious that you increase the risk of making mistakes and becoming distracted if you are multitasking as you present.

Recruit someone to take on the role of producer or technical support during your presentation. Let that person manage the tools, monitor incoming communication and eliminate other potential distractions so that you can commit your entire focus to delivering your message and engaging your audience.

ATTENTION SPANS ARE . . . HEY, WHAT'S THAT?

Once you grab the attention of the audience, launch an all-out effort to maintain that attention or keep pulling them back into the presentation. Attention spans are short. The brain has enormous capacity. It is nearly impossible for the human brain to stay focused on one topic or one person for an extended period of time. Attention span studies suggest that undivided attention capacity is between 15 and 30 seconds.

Thinking that you can maintain the attention of an audience for an extended period of time is wishful thinking. The goal, then, becomes to continually reengage the audience.

Because attention spans are short, we have to be incredibly efficient with our time. The next segment of this book, "Keep It Moving," focuses on ways to keep the presentation from getting bogged down. A presentation that bogs down is a dying presentation. You simply cannot allow this to happen. You will lose the audience. If outside forces are responsible for slowing the pace, find some way to change the pace. Downtime is an invitation for the collective brains in the audience to move on to something more interesting.

You've got his undivided attention.

You've lost it.

In the battle for the attention of your audience, remember three things:

1) It is difficult to distract someone who is completely engrossed in what they're doing.

2) If your information is interesting enough, you will maintain the audience's attention longer and recapture their attention more frequently.

3) Multitaskers are constantly distracted by irrelevant information and constantly scanning for new information. Their attention spans are subject to every piece of information that enters their realm. By allowing them to multitask, you are conceding any chance of instilling your message below a surface level.

Keep in mind that we are in a constant battle for the attention of the audience—which can be easily distracted. Do your best to incorporate activities in your virtual presentations that offer variety, choice, rapid responses and active and interactive learning. And never forget to keep it relevant.

Relentlessly incorporate techniques that will keep your remote audiences engaged. It takes planning and it takes some resourcefulness on your part. But it truly is a mind-set. Once your planning process consistently includes these concepts, the odds of being more interesting than any of the distractions will increase significantly.

CHAPTER 7
DON'T FLY SOLO

"The full benefit of virtual meetings can't be realized without letting go and allowing people to contribute openly and candidly."
—Gerard Lithgow, Cisco Systems

PREPARING AND DELIVERING a virtual presentation can add a significant amount of work to your already overloaded plate. So, for more efficient planning and execution, solicit help. You've probably heard the fun fact that a single horse can pull 6 tons of weight, but two horses together can pull 36 tons, or six times the weight that one horse can pull. I'm not comparing you to a horse. But when you have your normal workload plus the sole ownership of putting together, delivering and following up on a virtual presentation, you may feel as if you're pulling 36 tons of responsibility.

Rather than trying to pull off the entire meeting yourself, have members of your team or invited guests deliver some of the information with you. Give these individuals clear guidance and direction so they can be thorough and efficient in their preparation. When given specific directions and the proper tools, they won't need long to prepare.

John was determined to go solo . . . and he succeeded.

Most of the top radio and television talk show hosts don't fly solo. Most of them have cohosts, sidekicks, guests, callers or a cast of characters who make the show more interesting. Some of the best-known radio personalities rely on other voices to make the show more appealing to the listeners. Only someone with remarkable talent can carry a show all by himself or herself.

On the radio show *Car Talk*, the interaction between Click and

Clack, the Tappet Brothers, is what makes the show entertaining and engaging, even for those who have no interest in car repairs. Would the show be as popular if it was just Click or just Clack answering listeners' questions? I doubt it. More than 2 million listeners tune into *Car Talk* every week. Most listeners are not hoping to hear the solution to their engine problem. Most, including me, listen for the entertaining banter between the two brothers, Tom and Ray Magliozzi, and their callers. Even if you don't own a car, it's an entertaining show.

THE TEAM THAT PRESENTS TOGETHER, BONDS TOGETHER

Being asked to be a part of a virtual presentation team should be viewed as an opportunity, not a burden. And by requiring team members to take an active role in your meetings, you will develop a team that

- Feels more informed and more connected to the success of the business.
- Has a better understanding of the direction of the business, as well as the challenges, the competition and the opportunities that exist.
- Is given a continuous stream of opportunities to demonstrate communication, organization and leadership skills.
- Has a higher level of confidence.
- Will collectively become more effective leaders.
- Has a strong chemistry.

Make each meeting a team event where multiple people have a stake in the outcome. If people don't feel they have ownership, if they don't feel involved, if they don't feel that it is relevant to them, then they are going to tune out. Worse yet, they begin to see your virtual meetings as opportunities to get other things done.

Getting several people involved in your meeting spreads the work. No one individual feels smothered with the task of doing more than she can handle.

If you are going to require your team members to contribute to the presentations, your task is to provide the participants with clear, well-defined role descriptions and a detailed outline that enables them to quickly and efficiently organize and deliver their presentations. Make it easy for them to prepare so they don't perceive their involvement as an additional cross they have to bear on your behalf.

Later in this chapter I provide descriptions of six roles that you can assign to members of your team or participants in your virtual presentations. Use these role descriptions, or come up with your own collection of roles that will best serve your presentation objectives and your virtual audiences.

If you are assigning these roles, be sure to send each person assuming a role the following forms to help them prepare:

- Role description (found later in this chapter)
- The Virtual Prep Sheet and Sequencing Chart
- The meeting agenda
- Role Guidelines form (optional)

Once your team is familiar with the roles, you no longer need to send the role description. Send the Role Guidelines form if you feel the presenter needs additional guidance. You can also communicate these instructions via email or a phone call.

The person charged with executing the role should use the preparation and sequencing forms to prepare their message and to list the audio/visual support they will need. They should relay this information to the meeting leader. The leader can use it to prepare and further guide the presenter, if necessary.

Give your role players the best chance to succeed. Success leads to confidence. Confidence will lead to team members who are willing to take an active role in future meetings.

ROLE: PRODUCER

In chapter 2 ("Virtual Presentations Are Anything but New") we discussed some of the roles in the broadcasting industry. Remember, the producer owns the show. The producer is responsible for making sure that what is supposed to happen, happens.

As the producer of a virtual presentation, you will be involved to whatever extent the presenter or meeting leader needs you to be involved. You can assist in various aspects of the preparation phase. You can help during the presentation. You can take care of coordinating the follow-up communication with the participants.

The motto of the producer is "whatever it takes." Do whatever it takes to reduce the multitasking burden of the presenter. Let the presenter be the presenter. Provide support wherever it is needed, from developing the slide deck, to checking audio and video links, to ensuring that participants get connected, to sending out pre-meeting materials and agendas, to helping the participants understand how to participate in the presentation.

Having a producer makes the virtual presenter's life a lot easier. For the presenter, it means

- Starting the presentation with confidence that everything is in order.

- Continuing the presentation while the producer tends to and eliminates technical glitches.

- Knowing that after the presentation, the right follow-up material will get to the right people.

A good producer is worth his or her weight in gold. If the role of the producer is executed properly, the presenter will be free to concentrate on delivering a presentation that creates maximum impact for the audience.

ROLES: HOST AND COHOST

Host

The www.dictionary.com definition of a *host* is:

1. a person who receives or entertains guests at home or elsewhere

2. a master of ceremonies, moderator, or interviewer for a television or radio program.

Other names used for the *host* include, but are not limited to, *leader, director, conductor, chief, boss, person in charge, guide.*

> The discipline of the leader will determine the destiny of the meeting.

If you are hosting the virtual presentation, you are responsible for the entire meeting. You can delegate responsibilities, but the buck stops with you.

The host is responsible for three areas:

1. Pre-meeting

- Why are we doing this? —Define the purpose and necessity of the meeting.
- What do we need to cover? —Select and sequence the topics.
- Who should be involved? —Determine the participants and assign roles.
- How should we deliver it? —Organize the logistics: technology, tools, timing and connections.

2. During the meeting

   The host is responsible for delivering the information. The host can fly solo or fly in tandem with other presenters who prepare and deliver segments of the presentation.

3. Post-meeting

   Follow-up —Oversee the assembly and distribution of follow-up material.

Your role as the host is to create an atmosphere that is comfortable, conducive to effective exchanges of information and ideas and informative for the participants. Create a forum in which people freely contribute. Establish ground rules and procedures. Help the participants feel proficient at using the tools that will be available to them during the presentation.

Cohost

Some other names for the *cohost* include, among others, sidekick, companion, coanchor, right-hand person, shadow, twin, color commentator, wingman and backup.

Enlisting a cohost is one of the smartest and most effective ways to create a more interesting experience for the audience and for the host. A cohost can turn a potential monologue into a conversation. Having a cohost will relieve some of the pressure and responsibilities of the presenter. The cohost should share in handling the responsibilities of the host.

Adding a cohost to a virtual presentation will

- Make listening more interesting for the audience.
- Create an atmosphere that makes others want to join in.
- Add personality, humor and additional insights.
- Divide the preparation time, the presentation time and the responsibilities.
- Bring spontaneity to the presentation.
- Make it easier to insert questions and comments.
- Give each host additional time to gather thoughts.
- Allow for more consistent monitoring of questions, polls and surveys.
- Help vary the pace and tempo of the presentation.

"That is a fascinating point, Betty." "Hey, Jerry, we have more audience questions."

It is easier to communicate and coordinate the efforts of the host and cohost when they are in the same location. However, having a remote cohost is better than flying solo, even though the coordination is more difficult.

The involvement of a remote cohost requires some additional planning. It requires better coordination of the shared roles. Both hosts need to be in sync as to the sequencing and timing of the presentation. Shared responsibility requires more practice with the tools. This is especially true if there is any lag time with the audio. Things can sound disorganized very quickly when the hosts continuously step on each other: "You go ahead." "No, you go." "No, I didn't mean to cut you off, go ahead." "Sorry, didn't hear that, what did you say?" "I said, go ahead." "Sure . . . what were we talking about?"

This sort of stop-and-start delivery is going to happen occasionally, no matter how well you prepare. Work to avoid it for the sake of your perceived preparedness and for the comfort of your audience. These exchanges can quickly cause your participants to roll their eyes and go check to see if they have any new email messages to catch up on.

ROLE: FACILITATOR

A facilitator is a person assigned the role of leading a group to the achievement of a specific objective. The role of a facilitator can range from leading an entire meeting, presiding over a panel discussion or debate and guiding participants through a particular segment or topic discussion, to conducting a question-and-answer session and coordinating the introduction of presenters, topics and agenda items.

Some other names for the *facilitator* include *moderator, referee, broker, intermediary* and *discussion-coordinator*.

Synonyms for *facilitate* include *smooth the progress of, help, aid, assist, make possible, make easy.* These synonyms provide you with your directive. Create an environment in which communication, sharing and cooperation are unencumbered. Remove any barriers or impediments to dialogue and interaction.

With your guidance, the participants and panelists will contribute freely and openly to the event. Encourage participation and open sharing of information and ideas. You should understand enough about the topic to challenge ideas, ask good follow-up questions, continue a line of questioning, redirect the conversation or summarize what has been said.

As the facilitator, you must be enthusiastic throughout the session. Your energy will be contagious. Your body language, voice, tone and demeanor should invite people to relax and join in. Don't allow one or two individuals to dominate the conversation when it is more advantageous for the audience to hear a variety of viewpoints.

Be passionate, be efficient and always be professional.

Like the host, the facilitator has responsibilities in three areas:

1. Pre-meeting

    - Define the purpose—What do you strive to achieve during this segment?
    - Craft your opening 60–90 seconds by completing the Virtual Prep Sheet.
    - Use the Sequencing Chart to determine the topics, timing, tools and flow.
    - Study up on the topic, even if you know it quite well.
        - Find facts, research studies and articles that can add insight and depth to your segment.
        - Decide which tools are available and which tools you want to use during your segment.

- Find out who will assist you to connect participants, manage the tools and monitor polls and questions.

- Practice in order to make sure that the technology and tools are working properly.

- Get the names of all participants and their locations.

- Provide the participants with your agenda.

- Inform the participants prior to the presentation about what you expect of them.

- Determine how you will follow up with the participants and what they will receive.

To facilitate panel discussions and question-and-answer sessions:

- Contact the panelists and contributing participants.
  - Inform them about the topic.
  - Inform them as to what they need to be prepared to discuss.
  - Make sure they understand the purpose of the discussion in light of the overall meeting objectives.

- Talk with the panelists to get a feel for their understanding of the topic.
  - Tell them why they were selected to be on the panel.
  - Get a feel for their communication style and comfort level. (Do they ramble? Do you have to draw them out? How well do they communicate? Will they need more information?)
  - Provide access and direction to reference materials.
  - Provide access (if appropriate) to webinars, webcasts or podcasts they can view to gain a better understanding of the meeting flow, timing, topic and audience.

- Make sure they understand how much time is allotted to the discussion. For example, say, "Jerry, we have 12 minutes for our panel discussion. Keep your responses brief, 90 seconds or less. We simply don't have time for long responses during this segment. Please be succinct."

- Provide the panelists with a list of topics and questions to review prior to the meeting.

- Request that the panelists provide follow-up material to the participants. For example, say, "Because it is not possible to thoroughly cover this topic in the allotted time, Susan, please provide follow-up material that you think will help the participants gain a better working knowledge of the topic (articles, studies, websites or resources)."

If you will be introducing people as part of your role, ask each person you are introducing to send you a two-paragraph introduction listing the items they feel are important for the audience to know. The introduction should include something about them personally and professionally. The introduction should also include the purpose for their involvement on the panel.

Keep all introductions brief. Practice these presentations out loud. A well-delivered introduction will build the credibility of the panelists and set the tone for the discussion.

2. During the meeting

- Introduce the topic and its relevance to the participants. (If you don't know the relevance, ask the meeting leader.)

- Introduce the panelists—State their name, title, expertise and the reason each is on the panel.

- Begin the discussion. (Use the Sequencing Chart to map out the flow of the discussion points.)

- Direct the questions and the follow-up questions.

- Keep the discussion relevant.

  - Be prepared to redirect the discussion.

  - Be prepared to refocus a panelist if she gets off track.

- Clarify statements and questions.

- Spread the discussion points and questions among the panelists. Don't go in the same order for panelist comments every time. Mix it up.

3. After the meeting

- Provide follow-up material to both the participants and the panelists.

- Summarize the discussion points and conclusions.

- Personally thank the panelists for their participation in the meeting. This thank-you should occur twice: prior to the conclusion of the meeting and as a follow-up to the meeting via an email, phone call or handwritten note.

ROLE: TECH SUPPORT

The role of tech support is to ease the technical burden of the presenters and the participants. If the tech support role is executed properly, the technology used for the presentation will seem to disappear.

Some other names for a *tech support person* include *A/V person, technical guru, geek squad, IT, techie* and *brainiac*.

The tech support person's job is to provide assistance with anything related to the use of technology and any audio/visual components of the virtual presentation. The tech support role does not have to be filled by someone who is a *certified* techie with an extensive work history as a creator of animated feature films at Pixar. This person should have a working knowledge of the technology that will be used during the presentation and should understand how to use the tools that the presenter plans to incorporate during the presentation.

One thing that planning cannot prevent is a technological meltdown. Having a tech support person available throughout the presentation will minimize the downtime and damage that a meltdown can cause. The presenter will be able to continue the presentation while tech support resolves the issue.

Tech support people can do things such as make sure participants get connected to the meeting; check to see that drivers and software are functioning properly; and ensure that everything that is supposed to show up on the screen actually shows up on the screen. They also can connect call-ins; conduct and monitor polls and surveys; arrange for remote teams to communicate with each other during breakout discussions; and read incoming questions and communicate important information to the presenter via voice, text, hand signals, Instant Messaging (IM) or emoticons. The tech support person should eliminate distractions, help to manage the clock and provide reminders and cues to the presenter(s).

Another role of tech support is to aid the participants with instructions and guide them in their use of features and functions during the presentation. Many people, customers and employees included, are unfamiliar or uncomfortable with certain technology. They don't use it every day and feel a bit intimidated by it. They need someone to guide them through even the simplest steps.

The inability of participants to use the tools can be embarrassing, frustrating and even humiliating, enough so that some people will completely avoid it. This avoidance does not bode well for the presentation. The presenter has an important message to share with the audience. The audience must be able to follow the material and to be engaged in the presentation. If the audience dreads using the technology, they are less likely to fully participate in the presentation.

You've probably participated in online meetings that included a brief scripted technology tutorial at the start of the meeting. This tutorial was designed to get the participants comfortable with the tools being used. However, once the tutorial was over, you and the other participants were on your own to figure out what buttons to push and how to participate in the meeting. The scripted voice with the instructions was never heard from again.

Tech support should remain in the presentation until it is completed. Tech support should step in, when needed, to clarify instructions, answer operational questions and help make the presentation a productive experience for everyone involved.

Assigning a tech support person will enable the presenter to focus on delivering a message and engaging the audience instead of multitasking and being sidetracked by the technology during the presentation.

ROLE: REPORTER

A reporter is responsible for organizing and presenting information on a specific topic. The reporter owns the segment and is responsible for its content.

The role of a reporter is just like the role of reporters you see on newscasts. The person in this role should prepare beyond the immediate report and be able to add insights and answer questions.

For the most part, the reporter will complete the presentation before responding to questions. This does not, however, have to be the case.

The reporter has the ability to conduct interviews, add audio and visual elements, and use any other resources that will make the report more interesting and relevant. These reports can be delivered on location, or they can be conducted remotely.

If you are hosting a meeting and you need someone to report on a specific topic, remember what we said in chapter 2 ("Virtual Presentations Are Anything but New"):

"If a reporter has personal experience with the topic, a solid understanding of the topic and an emotional connection with the topic, then it will be a more interesting and enlightening story for the audience. If a reporter finds a topic interesting, it is easier for her to make the story interesting to the audience."

Be prepared. Keep your remarks brief. Stay on topic.

Use the talent that surrounds you to make your virtual presentations more interesting. There are many benefits to actively involving other people in your presentations. Your presentations will be more entertaining and there will be less pressure on you. The amount of preparation will be divided and shared. Your team will bond. Your team members will be given the opportunity to shine. And you will be delivering better presentations.

As the song goes, "One is the loneliest number . . ." So whenever possible, don't fly solo.

ROLE GUIDELINES

Meeting: _Regional managers meeting_   Date: _June 2_

Time: _4:00pm–4:45pm_   Meeting type: _Webinar_

Person: _Chris_   Role: _Reporter and Q&A Facilitator_

Topic: _Acme contract_

Segment objective: _Inform the managers about the status of the Acme contract. The key take-away point is that the contract is secure._

Time allotment: _4 minutes for your report. 6 minutes for Q&A._

Provided for you: _Agenda and attendee list, Virtual Prep Sheet and Sequencing Chart. Use the last two to organize._

Follow-up: _Provide a summary of your report and any pertinent information discussed during Q&A._

Additional information and suggestions: _During Q&A ask Kathy to comment on the contract. She's worked with Acme over the last 18 months. Her insights will benefit the team._

Keep it relevant. Keep it engaging. Keep it moving.
- Take pride in your segment.
- Do not exceed your allotted time.
- Practice improves: confidence, content, delivery and timing.

CHAPTER 8
DEVELOP A DYNAMIC, PROFESSIONAL ON-SCREEN PRESENCE

TO BECOME AN EXCEPTIONAL VIRTUAL PRESENTER, you must develop an on-screen presence that appears confident, relaxed and commanding. Because of the additional challenges and barriers thrown at you when presenting virtually, you have to demonstrate better presentation skills than when the audience is in the same room with you.

What you are wearing, your body language and facial expressions, your movements and gestures all communicate a message as to your level of confidence and professionalism.

LOOK RELAXED AND CONFIDENT

Generally, someone who looks relaxed appears confident. Any time you are visible on the screen, you are projecting nonverbal messages to your audience. What impression do you want to make? Your on-screen presence will go a long way in establishing and reinforcing your credibility. It will set the audience's level of expectation and will play a significant role in how effective you will be in delivering your message.

The vast majority of the virtual presentations involve sitting in front of a camera, either at a desk or a table. Some virtual presentation tools allow the presenter to stand and move, but for the purpose of our discussion, we will focus on techniques for being a more effective presenter when you are seated.

An additional restriction when you are presenting virtually is that the video screen limits what the audience can see. In contrast, face-to-face presentations have the advantage of allowing the audience to see a wider and more inclusive picture of the presenter and his surroundings.

🔌 Make it appear as if you are in the same room.

In creating an in-person atmosphere for your presentation, avoid looking like a talking head on a computer screen. Rather, set the stage to appear as if you are sitting across the table from the audience. To do this, assume a posture that is relaxed but attentive. Look alert, engaged and eager to communicate your message. It's hard to appear fully engaged if you are leaning back in your chair or leaning in so close to the camera that your face fills the entire picture frame. Assume a position that allows you to use your hands freely to emphasize key points.

You will look more engaged if you rest your hands about 8 to 12 inches on the table in front of you. Have most of your forearms on the table, but keep your elbows off the table to prevent you from leaning on them, which causes your shoulders to appear hunched.

Look relaxed yet attentive. Place your hands 8 to 12 inches on the table in front of you.

Avoid T-Rex—sitting with your hands on the edge of the table—which can make even the most formidable presenter appear a bit pensive and unengaged.

USE GESTURES EFFECTIVELY AND AVOID THE *DESPERATE HANDS* SYNDROME

Don't limit your expressions to just your face, your eyes and your voice. Research conducted at the University of Missouri by Janet Iverson showed that gestures are a result of our desire to express ourselves. We're born with a propensity to use our hands when we speak.

🔌 Use gestures that reinforce your message.

There are three ways that on-screen gestures differ from in-person gestures:

1) Hand movements are more pronounced on the screen than they are in person. Because you are framed within a limited area, all of your movements are more pronounced. Frequent hand movements and hands that flash in and out of the frame can be distracting. If the video is choppy because of the online connections, then you probably want to limit your hand movements in order to reduce the distractions that result from flailing hands.

2) When your hands get too close to the camera, they appear larger than they are in proportion to the rest of your image. Be sure to keep your hands from getting too close to the camera.

Big hand = ineffective   Effective

3) Hands that move excessively appear desperate.

What do I mean by the term *desperate hands*? Here's an example. I was working with a client in New York City who was preparing for a virtual presentation. I was videotaping his presentation so that we could review the video and make adjustments to both his content and his delivery style. His image was framed in the camera the same as it would be during his virtual presentation.

Desperate hands

After reviewing 3 minutes of the video, the client shouted: "Look at my hands! They look desperate." He proceeded to say that his hands looked out of control. He said that the continuous, excessive flailing made him appear desperate, instead of reinforcing his image as a highly educated, experienced consultant. His flailing hands were serving as a distraction instead of serving to reinforce his message.

Don't fidget.

People tend to fidget when they are uncomfortable, nervous, anxious, overly eager or not confident about the information they are presenting. Fidgety hands also show up during question-and-answer sessions, when the pressure is on or the tough question hangs in the air.

When your hands are separated, they can't fidget with each other. If your hands are empty, they have nothing to fidget with. If you have to hold a pen or marker in your hand, keep it still. Don't click the cap, twirl it like a baton or spin it like a helicopter blade on your hand. If the pen becomes a source of your fidgeting, then set it down, unless you need it to write something down.

If you are going to use your hands to express yourself, be specific. Use well-defined gestures. The more defined your hands appear, the more defined your message will appear to your audience. Here are illustrations that demonstrate effective gestures that remain within the frame of the video.

If you have read my book *The Exceptional Presenter*, these gestures will be familiar to you. My question is, are you using them to reinforce your points and to appear more confident? If not, here is another chance to develop the skill of using effective gestures that will heighten your ability to influence, inform and persuade others. Well-executed gestures will help your audiences visualize your message.

When emphasizing numbers

"There are two areas of concern."

"Five years ago this technology didn't exist."

"Let's not worry about that."

"Our Dallas distributor can handle those issues."

When giving instructions and locations

"The Claw" (illustrated above) is a versatile and strong-looking gesture.

When using verbs

"Market share has increased from 12 percent to 18 percent."

"We've increased our efficiency."

"We've decreased our expenses."

When showing comparisons

"What used to take 9 months, now takes 6 months."

"You're looking to downsize from 50,000 square feet to 30,000 square feet."

When stating dates or timelines

"We started in January and finished in June."

"You should move the project publication date from August to September."

"The project began last November."

When giving chronological sequences

"The project will end by January of next year."

Perform chronological gestures in the direction that the audience reads, from *their* left to *their* right.

EYE CONTACT IS ALWAYS CRITICAL

Even though you are miles away from your audience members, you can still use eye contact to connect with them. Staring at the camera lens makes it difficult to concentrate, so try looking beyond the lens and visualize your audience. Making eye contact can seem a bit awkward in virtual settings, but with practice, you will become more comfortable with it.

Just as your hand movements can appear more pronounced on the screen, so can your eye movements. The closer your face is to the camera, the more exaggerated your eye movements appear. The slightest eye movements can appear more prominent than they really are.

Move back from the screen. If your camera is positioned so that your image on the screen includes the top of your head down to the desk in front of you, slight eye movements are barely noticeable.

News anchors read a teleprompter that is built into the studio camera. Because of the distance from the camera and the slight head movements the anchors make while speaking, television viewers can't tell that they are reading.

Vary your targets when making eye contact.

Please keep in mind that you do not have to stay focused on the camera throughout the entire presentation. In normal face-to-face interactions, people look at many things. If someone were to stare at you the entire duration of a one-on-one meeting, you would probably feel uncomfortable. It is normal to look at your notes, glance to the side or look at what is on the screen. If there are other people in the room with you, direct some of your eye contact to them. Doing so makes the presentation appear more like an in-person presentation than one being conducted digitally.

Reminder: Look at the camera as you practice your presentation. The more you do this, the more comfortable you will become doing it. Do it enough times, and it will start to feel normal.

YOUR *VIRTUAL VOICE* MUST SOMETIMES CARRY THE MESSAGE

On a phone call, conference call, webinar or any time you are presenting without the aid of video, your voice is the transport system for your message. It is your only physical tool to carry your message to the audience. Therefore, in virtual settings, when you are not visible to the audience, you need to have greater command of your voice.

> Let your confidence and enthusiasm flow through your voice.

Your *virtual voice* should be

- **Dynamic**—Stretch the range of your voice. Avoid falling into a monotone vocal range. Monotone and virtual don't mix. You have enough of a battle on your hands to keep the attention of the audience. A monotone voice will drive them to distractions.

- **Animated**—Sound excited about your material and eager to pass it along to the audience.

- **Easy to hear**—Adding volume to your voice will make it easier for the audience to hear and understand the presentation. This doesn't mean yelling into the microphone. Some people feel compelled to yell because the audience is so far away.

- **Articulate**—Because speakers and microphones are not always top quality, you must pay particular attention to articulating your words. Use pauses frequently to delineate thoughts and ideas. An audience quickly grows frustrated when listening to a mumbling voice.

If you think the audience may have missed something or misunderstood something that was said, repeat it. This is absolutely necessary in virtual meetings because oftentimes audience members will not let you know that they didn't hear something. It is easier for them to stay quiet than to speak up. On the other hand, if you are participating in a meeting and you can't hear something that is said, ask the person presenting the information to repeat what was said. If you didn't hear it, others probably didn't hear it either.

Eliminate verbal graffiti— completely.

Verbal graffiti—the "ums" and "uhs"—stand out more in virtual presentations because they are spoken directly into the microphone. Verbal graffiti does not sound professional. It makes us sound unprepared, hesitant and somewhat uninformed.

President Barak Obama is an outstanding orator. He is better, however, when he is reading his speeches from a teleprompter than when he is speaking extemporaneously. His vocal tempo changes dramatically when he is not using a teleprompter to read his speech. Much of the authority and command in his voice goes away when he is speaking off-the-cuff.

The usage of the nonword "uh" by President Obama jumps dramatically when he is responding to questions or speaking without a script. How many times did President Obama use "uh" and "um" during his inaugural speech, his first bicameral speech to Congress and the first 10 minutes of his first White House press conference combined? Zero. All of those speeches were read from a teleprompter. The speech team doesn't insert "um" and "uh" into any of the president's written speeches.

During the first three answers to the first three questions of his first White House press conference, President Obama used the verbal graffiti "uh" and "um" a grand total of 143 times. Can his tempo, pace and conviction be as effective when he injects "uh" and "um" 143 times into three answers? No.

We should never allow verbal graffiti to diminish our impact. Be alert for other variations of verbal graffiti such as "you know," "to be honest with you," "like," "frankly," and "basically."

By recording your practice sessions, you will have the opportunity to listen for and eliminate your verbal graffiti. Learn to pause instead of inserting "um" or "uh." Once you are aware of the verbal graffiti that you tend to use, try to avoid it, 24 hours a day, 7 days a week. Don't use it in casual conversations, phone calls, meetings, voice mail or virtual interactions. Once you have eliminated verbal graffiti from your vocabulary, you will not want it back. You won't miss it. Your audience certainly won't miss it either.

USE STORIES AND EXAMPLES

If your audience can't see you, be sure to use visually descriptive examples and stories to help your audience *see* the point of your story. If your audience cannot see your facial expressions, body language or gestures, your descriptions and stories should be more vivid and detailed.

Stories and examples are easier for the audience to visualize than are theories, numbers, statistics and scripted text. Stories are more interesting to listen to and easier to follow. Your voice will be much more conversational and animated when you are telling a story than when you are simply disseminating information. Always keep in mind that your stories and examples should be directly on topic, short and to the point. Don't waste time telling stories or using examples that are not relevant.

Don't tell stories just to tell stories. Share personal stories and experiences. Share stories that you have read in periodicals and books and seen on television and heard on radio broadcasts. If you have a specific topic in mind as you read and listen, you will be amazed at how many stories relate to that topic.

Storytelling is fun and entertaining. But if your stories become excessive or excessively long, they lost their purpose.

USE PROPS AND ARTICLES AS VISUAL AIDS

Using current periodicals, props, product samples and other visual aids during your virtual presentation can help to maintain the attention of your audience, if done properly. There is one major difference when using these items during a virtual presentation as opposed to using them when everyone is in the room. Most of the time, the quality of the picture doesn't allow for your virtual audience to see the detail of the item that you are displaying. For example, if you hold up the front page of the *Wall Street Journal* to highlight an article you are using to reinforce a point, someone sitting across a conference table would at least be able to read the headline. In a virtual setting, this is probably not the case. For your audience to have the slightest chance of reading it, the picture quality has to be high definition. You can reference the article during a virtual presentation, but you have to provide more specifics as to what the article is about and how it relates to your message. Unless you are using high-definition cameras and screens, don't assume that the audience can see the detail of anything you are holding up to display.

When using props and articles during your virtual presentations, be assertive, be deliberate and make sure your audience understands the connection between the prop and your message.

Ineffective   Effective

Your on-screen presence will impact audience expectations, your professional image and your reputation as a virtual meeting leader. Practice your virtual presentation delivery skills. More time practicing will translate to more effective and consistent delivery skills.

Most presenters never even think about the basic skills you are reviewing in this book. Most are not concerned about improving the way they present. For that matter, most presenters have no desire to review or critique their delivery style or level of effectiveness. They just keep presenting the way they have always presented. This creates a bad scenario for these individuals when they deliver virtual presentations because virtual presentations require a more complete set of delivery skills.

If you record and critique your virtual presentations, be assured that you will improve. A 10 percent improvement in your delivery skills could make the difference between a run-of-the-mill presentation and an exceptional presentation.

CHAPTER 9
CREATE AN IN-PERSON EXPERIENCE

THE ATMOSPHERE FOR YOUR VIRTUAL PRESENTATION will affect the feel and flow of the meeting. Is it hectic and hurried, or is it calm and in control? Does it create an "I-want-to-be-part-of-this" attitude, or does it make your participants stare at the clock just waiting for the session to be over?

A setting that looks familiar to the participants will elevate their comfort level. They will be more relaxed and at ease. They will be more likely to participate, contribute and stay involved and will generally be more open to ideas and information. They will smile more easily and be more comfortable when sharing their opinions. They will tend to drop their barriers and be less guarded.

> 🔌 The goal is to create a presentation atmosphere that appears to be as much like a face-to-face meeting as possible.

Your job, then, is to do whatever it takes to make your presentation setting look like a working session and not a head shot you would take in a photo booth at the mall, with the forced head tilt and fake background. Your desk should look as it normally looks—minus the mess. Display such items as your notes, a notepad and your coffee cup or water glass. If you are going to use a prop to make a point, such as a magazine, keep it readily available on the table. It's your space. Use it as you would during an in-person meeting.

GET OUT OF MY FACE!

Blog entry from John in Orlando, Florida

I was attending a virtual user conference in Orlando. Midway through the conference, it was apparent that one of the presenters was not going to show up. Being a member of the conference committee and having some experience with the topic, I volunteered to fill in for the missing expert—a noble decision on my part, but a hasty one indeed.

Things seemed to go pretty well. I had enough material to fill the 30-minute slot, and I didn't pass out, so I was pleased. I was pleased, that is, until I saw the recording of my presentation 2 weeks later posted on the website for the entire world to see. What I saw was embarrassing. My face could not have been any closer to the camera. It looked huge. It was painful to watch. All I saw were darting eyeballs, teeth and nose hair. Most of the audience members were watching the conference on 6-foot wide, ultra-high-definition screens. I can only imagine what they were thinking during my presentation. 💬

The typical view of a presenter in a virtual meeting is the extreme close-up, or what I call the *way too close-up*. The camera is angled up, and the imposing face is staring down at the participants. Comedian Jerry Seinfeld refers to this as the *close talker*. It's what you saw on the playground at recess when the bully was standing over you, staring down and demanding your milk money. Remember that image?

The "way too close-up."

It's interesting how people thousands of miles away can violate your personal space. In face-to-face business interactions, we have a better sense as to how close we should stand in relation to another person. The distance is based on personal relationships, cultural differences and familiarity. In virtual presentations, the person in your space seems oblivious to the effect at the other end of the digital connection. From such close range the eyes appear to dart all over the screen. The slightest eye movements are magnified to the point of distraction. The presenter glances at the camera, then to the slide, then to his notes, and then back to the camera.

There is a simple fix to eliminate the *way too close-up* position. Place the camera at eye level and move it back. The eye level placement of the camera will help to create the appearance of a face-to-face, one-on-one conversation and will prevent you from looking down at your audience. You can set your computer monitor or camera on just about anything to raise it to eye level. By moving the camera farther away, you immediately eliminate most of the overly pronounced eye movements. The glances from the monitor to the camera and back are less noticeable.

Keep in mind that if your camera is attached to or built into your computer, when you move the camera farther away, you are moving the microphone away as well. Since maintaining good voice quality is important for your online presentations, choose your microphone carefully. Be sure the one you choose does not interfere with your ability to use your hands freely to gesture, operate the computer, flip through notes and use your props during the presentation. Cordless is an excellent option. Headsets and lapel microphones are both good choices as well. Speakerphones allow for hands-free access, but even the high-end speakerphones don't handle more than one voice at a time very effectively. Practice using different microphones to find out which one works best for your delivery style and which will work best for the interaction you plan to have with the audience.

Blog entry from Karen in New York, New York

I was on a conference call recently with 16 other people. The leader of the call did an excellent job of reviewing the information that was to be covered. The one big negative aspect of the meeting was the continuous trampling on participants' voices by the leader. The leader would ask a question and pause. It was uncanny how, as soon as someone spoke up, the leader would begin talking again. Neither the leader nor the person asking the question could hear one another. The rest of us on the call could hear both voices. Both the leader and the participant would talk for 30 seconds, not hearing a thing the other was saying. They would finish talking at about the same time. The leader had no idea a question had been asked, and the questioner had no idea that her question had not been heard.

Understandably, after this had happened two or three times, no one, including me, was willing to speak up. 💬

When you don't have visual contact with your audience, you need to establish a signal or pattern of speech that lets the audience know that you are about to begin speaking. Try something as simple as: "Are there further questions regarding our Q3 objectives? (Extended pause for 10–12 seconds) Any questions? (Pause for 4–5 seconds) With that (slight pause of 2–3 seconds, to see if anyone had started to ask a question), I will turn it over to Jeanne who will . . ." The first pause should be long enough so that a participant has the time to think of the question, switch off the mute button and begin speaking.

Camera placement, lighting, background and sound all impact the look and feel of your presentation.

MAKE IT LOOK AS THOUGH YOU ARE IN THE SAME ROOM

In order to make your video-based presentation look as if you are in the same room with your audience, determine what will be visible in the frame. Make sure your image in the frame includes from a few inches above the top of your head to your hands resting on the table or desk. This is what people sitting across a table from you see when they meet with you in person, so make it the same for someone watching you on the screen? By setting this as your scene, you create a more typical, in-person feel to your presentation. The camera is far enough away to de-emphasize your eye movements, and you can gesture more freely and naturally than when the camera is located close to your face. The close camera causes your hands to flash abruptly in and out of the tighter frame.

If you are a participant in the meeting and your image is small, move the camera closer so that the rest of the participants can see you more clearly. The postage stamp–size video shots are too small to allow you to include your head and torso in the frame. Preview what you will look like to the other participants. If you feel that the camera is too far away, then by all means, move it closer.

When you are presenting via telepresence or videoconference, you generally don't control what is in the frame. The rooms used for these meetings are arranged to look like high-end conference rooms. Some systems allow for panning and zooming of the camera, but for the most part, the scene is preset.

NOT GOOD   BETTER   BEST

Most of you probably don't have stylists, lighting specialists and makeup artists available to make you look good. You're on your own. If the professionals aren't available to make you look good, then positioning yourself a little farther away from the camera is the next best thing.

GOOD LIGHTING PREVENTS CREEPY FACES

Lighting is an important part of any photograph or video. The *way too close-up* position is a good example of bad lighting. Too many shadows are being cast in too many places. It creates a creepy, shadowy look that is not conducive to making your audience feel comfortable. In addition, the light from the computer screen can create sharp contrasts. Well-placed lighting can cancel many of the shadows on your face and generate a much more pleasant visual image.

Here are three simple suggestions to improve the lighting and thus improve your on-screen look:

1) Search the Internet for websites that provide lighting instructions for your video casts. You will find many sources that will offer advice for your lighting needs. It's

not expensive to light your scene properly, but it is an important step in creating an in-person experience.

2) Pay a local photographer to spend an hour with you to discuss the various lighting options. If you conduct webcasts and other video presentations from your office, have the photographer provide specific lighting setup instructions for the space. This way, you can place your monitor or camera in the same place every time to create a consistent look to your presentations.

3) Set your computer screen saver to a much longer time interval before it activates or falls asleep. This will eliminate your image transitioning from light to dark and back to light again. The frequent changing of the lighting is distracting for you and for your audience. Setting the lighting of your screen to a dimmer setting can also reduce the visual impact when the lighting on your computer changes.

SET THE BACKGROUND SCENE

The background for your virtual presentations can vary widely. The important thing to think about is what you want the background to do. Do you want the background to go unnoticed? Do you want it to make a statement? Is there anything in the background that will distract your audience? What impression does it make?

Many different backgrounds will work. Unless you want your background to make a statement, stay neutral. I've seen presenters who are overshadowed by what is in the background, and others who are so good that the background fades away and goes unnoticed.

For business presentations, a background that looks professional will serve you well. Think about what a business office or conference room looks like, and replicate it.

Some people use green-, blue- or white-screen technology to create their background. This technology allows you to literally have any picture or scene behind you. If you want sand and surf in the background, you've got it. If you want video of the Capitol with flags waving, you've got it.

Avoid backgrounds that will draw the attention of your audience, such as people walking around, your cat grooming himself, or another computer monitor or television screen flickering. The light from a window in the background can compromise the image of the presenter or cause a continuously changing visual image as a result of changing sunlight.

Amy always seems so relaxed and prepared.

Wearing neutral-colored clothing works well because it creates less contrast with your image on the screen. Certain colors and patterns of clothing can make the screen flicker. Flowery, stripy, checkered and patterned shirts, jackets, dresses, blouses and ties can wreak havoc on some cameras. Flickering equates to distraction.

The great thing about virtual presentation

They have no idea how prepared she is.

technology is that you can test the camera and microphone prior to the actual online presentation. Experiment with different backgrounds. See how various clothing alternatives look on screen. Take the time to do this. It's your presentation, so be diligent about your lighting, your sound, your background and your attire. Make sure the image you are projecting is the one that you want others to see.

TO RECORD OR NOT TO RECORD

Most online meeting programs now allow you to record the session. There are many reasons you might want to record the presentation. Perhaps not everyone can attend because of time issues or prior obligations. Maybe you want to record the meeting so it can be shared with others or for training purposes.

Whatever the reason, the question remains: should you record the meeting or not?

> Recording a meeting creates a permanent event. There are no take backs.

Recording the meeting will impact the atmosphere, the flow of the meeting, and the level of participation. Recording the meeting will affect the level of candor and openness from the participants (perhaps even the leaders). Therefore, when deciding whether or not to record the meeting, ask yourself these questions:

- Will recording the meeting inhibit others' input and participation? If so, how important is their participation?

- Will participants feel free to speak openly without concern that their comments will someday come back to haunt them?

- In what ways will recording the meeting change the group dynamic?

- Is there any chance that the meeting will be seen by people other than those intended to see it or hear it?

- How much damage can be done if the recording of the meeting falls into the hands of a competitor? Would the answer to the previous question limit the information the group is willing to share at the meeting?

It would be unusual for anyone to behave completely naturally when everything that is said or done is being recorded. For some people, a video camera brings out the inner thespian. They see it as an opportunity to perform in the spotlight. All too often, however, it quickly becomes apparent to the other meeting participants why this person did not pursue acting as a profession. For others, camera time equals turtle time. They pull back into their shell and stay there until the danger passes or the meeting ends. They are keenly aware that any mistake they make during the presentation will remain in circulation indefinitely.

Recording your meeting will put a crimp in spontaneity.

One benefit of a meeting is the camaraderie that is built within the group. The stories and experiences that are shared, the good-natured kidding and teasing that goes on, the quick back-and-forth conversations, the off-the-cuff comments and the aha! moments all make for a more enjoyable event.

Do you lose these moments when everyone knows that everything is being recorded? Think about situations that *at the time* are particularly funny, entertaining or engaging but later on make no sense to the people who weren't there. Humor used *in the moment* might seem inappropriate when seen or heard at a different place and time. Kidding about the boss might seem harmless when everyone is present but might not seem funny to the boss as he watches the meeting 2 weeks later, by himself, in his office.

Here are two simple questions to answer to help you decide whether to record the meeting or not:

1) What do I gain by recording?

2) What might I lose by recording?

Weigh the pros and cons to help you decide which route to take.

Creating an in-person experience requires a more detailed level of planning and thought. Notice the things you experience during face-to-face presentations: the visuals, the sounds, the surroundings and the people. Try to replicate that experience. You can't replicate it exactly, but with the combination of planning, setup and a conversational and engaging delivery style, you can create an experience where your participants feel as though they're in the room with you.

CHAPTER 10
BE RESOURCEFUL

AS A MEETING PRODUCER, HOST, cohost, facilitator, tech support person or reporter, look for opportunities to bring freshness, spontaneity, enthusiasm, fun and a sense of anticipation to your presentation.

I was originally going to name this chapter "Be Creative." But being creative seems to demand too much time, thinking and risk taking. Why create something when you can use techniques that have already been proven to be successful?

So in the tradition of *keeping it simple*, I suggest that instead of spending your time and energy being creative, spend it being resourceful. Look around and see what other people are doing. In chapter 2 ("Virtual Presentations Are Anything but New"), we looked at what the broadcasting industry does, every day, to grab and hold your attention. Every technique used in broadcasting and every technique used in face-to-face presentations, for that matter, can be modified for your virtual presentations.

Being resourceful implies that you use the talents that exist within your team to create better online presentations. Tap into their talents. Take advantage of the knowledge and experience of your audience to build a better presentation. Being resourceful means looking beyond the ordinary to find interesting and productive ways to use the tools and talents that surround you.

Being resourceful doesn't mean that you have to use *off-the-wall* activities or tactics. Think of what your audience would be drawn to, and what is at your disposal. You don't need gimmicks to be interesting, although an occasional gimmick with the right audience can be fun.

> Most meetings are so bland that the audience will appreciate just about anything you do to bring energy, interest and excitement to the meeting.

Don't rely solely on technology to grab the attention of your audience. The current online technology offers a broad range of activities, resources and tools that can add animation and help to promote audience involvement. But if you are trying to *wow* them with the technology, think of what your presentations are being compared to, such as television programs that have expansive production budgets. With television, the action is nonstop as multiple-camera shots flash over the screen. Music, video, photos, color and light are all used to grab the viewer's attention. The amount of information and the number of edits spliced together for a single commercial can be mind-boggling. You can't compete with that, so don't even try.

Personalities are a key attraction in any presentation. If you replaced the cast in the television show *The Office* with the panelists from the show *Meet the Press*, do you think *The Office* would be as funny as it is? I'm betting that it wouldn't. Don't get me wrong. I like the panelists from *Meet the Press*, but I like them in that role. Television comedies typically require multiple episodes to gain momentum with viewers, because it takes viewers time to get familiar with and appreciate the personalities of the characters. Television comedies seem funnier when you feel connected to the characters. Part of the long-term popularity of *Meet the Press* can be attributed to the personalities of the hosts, guests and panelists.

If technology was the primary driver to keep people engaged, then radio would not exist. Radio doesn't offer any of the visual pizzazz of television, yet radio can be just as, if not more, captivating as television, again mainly due to the personalities involved.

PRESENTING TO AN INVISIBLE AUDIENCE

Presenting to an audience you can't see is not a new concept. You may not have thought about it, but you have a vast amount of experience communicating with remote audiences. How many hours have you spent on the telephone in your lifetime? Depending on your age, you have probably spent thousands of hours talking on the telephone. You were presenting to a remote audience during every one of those calls. Presenting to an invisible audience is not something that is foreign to you. The difference is that during virtual presentations you are presenting to more than one person, and you might not be able to hear the audience.

I'm often asked, "What's the best way to talk to an invisible audience?" My answer, "The same way you talk to your friends on the telephone." Speak to your audience during a virtual presentation the same way you speak during a lively phone conversation. Make it conversational and maintain an active vocal range that radiates confidence and enthusiasm.

When your audience is not present, it is more difficult to determine their disposition, interpret how they are feeling and get a sense of their comfort level. Sometimes you just don't know if your message is getting across to them. You don't have the visual clues that you have when you are face-to-face. Some of the clues come from their body language as well as their facial expressions, glances, raised eyebrows, the smirks or smiles and the eye contact—or lack thereof. A subtle headshake can indicate agreement, disagreement or confusion. A sweaty upper lip or forehead can be a sign that an audience member is uncomfortable or nervous or that the temperature in the room is too high. Audience members shifting in their seats may indicate that you need to change the pace, change the topic, take a break or get them involved.

The many nonverbal signs—such as body language, movements, eye contact and gestures of the audience—provide a definite advantage for in-person interactions. These visual clues are absent during some online presentations. However, just because we can't see the audience does not mean that we lose all of the clues that the audience is sending our way.

If you want to have any idea of what the audience thinks of your information, you have to make an effort to hear your audience by having them inject comments or respond to questions, polls and surveys.

PRESENTING TO A SILENT AUDIENCE

Silence can be golden, but it can also be awkward and uncomfortable. This is especially true during virtual meetings. You don't have the opportunity to read body language, facial expressions and eye contact, and you can't tell if the audience smiled or laughed at your attempted humor.

Good silence.

Bad silence.

As the leader of the meeting or segment, the silence could mean many things. It could mean that your audience is pondering the relevance of what you just said and taking copious notes, as you wax eloquently. However, it could also mean that they are involved in texting, emailing, doing laundry, watching television or chatting among themselves. They could be rolling their eyes at your comments or yelling at their muted telephone saying something like, "We know this already!" Or they might just be sitting there thinking, "This guy has no idea what he's talking about."

If you are not receiving verbal feedback, you have no way of knowing what your audience is doing or what they are thinking about. It's easy to get frustrated and even a bit irritated when you feel that people are not listening to you, that they're bored or they disagree with what you are saying. These feelings can be magnified when it appears to you that they're refusing to state their opinions or they're too lazy to "un-mute" their phone and make a comment.

> Silence can be deafening. It can dampen your enthusiasm. It can shake your confidence.

How can you break the silence? There are times during a virtual or face-to-face presentation when the audience is silent. The issue with virtual presentations is that when your audience is silent, they are completely silent. A muted audience is soundless. You don't hear anything: not a cough, not a paper rattling, not a clearing of the throat—nothing. Here are five surefire ways to break the silence.

#1 Add another voice by prerecording part of your presentation.

Many products are available that allow you to quickly and easily edit and modify audio and video clips, photos and commentary that you can embed into your Keynote or PowerPoint deck. Almost every smart phone has a record feature that will allow you to play back recordings during the presentation.

If you are sharing your desktop with the participants and you have Internet access, your audio and visual options have no limit. Use video clips that have already been created and are available online.

Placing a prerecorded segment in your presentation will also provide you with a few minutes of downtime in which you can gather your thoughts, conduct a poll or organize your next segment.

#2 Recruit a cohost or sidekick.

In chapter 7 ("Don't Fly Solo"), we defined the role of a cohost. A cohost immediately adds a second voice and creates a more interesting dynamic. This person will interact with you in a conversational way. The rest of the audience will hear the cohost make comments like, "Interesting," "Yes, that makes perfect sense," "U-m-m h-u-m-m" or "In addition to what Diane just said, I think it is important that we remember . . ." The audience will also hear the cohost laugh at the humorous things you say. It's easier to get others to laugh when they know the information was meant to be funny. When an audience hears laughter, the atmosphere becomes more relaxed. It sounds like a fun conversation to participate in.

A cohost makes the presentation easier and more comfortable for the host. This is the reason why so many television and radio shows include a host and a cohost or sidekick: the legendary team of Johnny Carson and Ed McMahon, Regis and Kelly, Howard Stern and his cast of many, and Mike Greenberg and Mike Golic of "Mike and Mike in the Morning" on ESPN radio. Even a soloist like Rush Limbaugh has a studio crew that he can interact with to make the show sound more like a conversation than a monologue.

It helps if your cohost has the same level of interest in the topic as you have because the mutual interest will create a genuine conversation that will be interesting to you, the cohost and the participants.

Blog entry from Tim Koegel, Washington, DC

Several years ago I was asked to lead a 90-minute webinar on the topic of presentation skills. My contact at the organization had read my book *The Exceptional Presenter* and had expressed great interest in its contents. He also happened to be a former radio host. Instead of doing the 90-minute webinar solo, I asked him to cohost the program. We discussed the timeline and items we needed to cover. His role was to make comments and ask questions whenever he felt compelled to do so. We established hand signals so I could let him know if he was taking too long with a question or comment and for when he should stay silent.

The webinar was a success. The 90 minutes felt like 15 minutes because of the easy, conversational flow and the genuine interaction that took place. All of the necessary material was covered. He asked great questions. He was also able to tie the benefits of the information directly to the audience because he works with the audience members every day. And we were able to share the responsibility of monitoring questions and polls during the webinar. I am certain that the webinar was more interesting to the audience because of the inclusion of a cohost.

#3 Plant questions and comments.

If, prior to the presentation, a participant tells you an interesting or relevant comment related to your topic, ask the person to make that same comment during your presentation.

If you know that some participants have expertise related to a topic, let them know that you will be asking them a question or two about that topic during the presentation. (You can even let them know what the questions will be.)

If you have an ally in the audience, ask her to be ready to add a comment or ask a question when it sounds as if you need some support or need time to gather your thoughts.

#4 Use forced participation.

The best way to break the silence is to invite others into your presentation. If they don't accept your invitation to join in, then it's time to prod them into participating. If they remain silent, it's time for forced participation.

Part of your pre-meeting preparation should be to alert the participants as to what they can expect and what is expected of them during the presentation. Let the participants know whether you will be calling on them directly or randomly during the presentation. Forced participation can serve to keep your audience alert.

Don't use forced participation to the point where your participants can't relax or where they are more stressed out about being called on than they are open to the information you are sharing. Use the available feedback options, such as applause, polls, surveys, questions and verbal responses, to bring your audience into the presentation.

If you are forcing audience members to participate, give them the best chance to succeed. There are few things worse than being humiliated or embarrassed in front of your peers because you were unprepared to answer a question tossed at you, unexpectedly, by the meeting leader.

Unless the presentation is strictly one-way (presenter to the audience), force someone to participate. Be sure to state their name prior to asking them a question or requesting a response. By doing so, you don't catch them off guard, and they don't become embarrassed because they didn't hear the question. As mentioned before, give the person a chance to succeed. The more times a member of the audience speaks up and something positive comes of it, the greater the chances that other audience members will also be willing to contribute during your session.

Blog entry from Cindy in Orlando, Florida

I was in a webinar being conducted by our main office. We had every region in the country on the webinar. Our regions are numbered. The meeting was conducted to discuss best practices within our division. The leader of the webinar could not get anyone to participate. His method went something like this, "OK, can I hear from Region E14." Silence would follow. He would move on. A few minutes later he would say, "Region W11, you had a great quarter. To what do you attribute your success?" Silence. He never asked any single individual, by name, to speak up. Unless someone was singled out, no one on the call was going to be the first to say anything. 💬

That meeting should have been archived in the "Worst Practices" vault.

#5 Use the *Super-Pause.*

Because it is more difficult to get the silent audience involved, you need to become comfortable with the Super-Pause. If you ask a question to a muted audience, it takes time for the audience members to process the question, formulate an answer and muster the courage to speak up.

Be prepared to pause for 15 to 20 seconds in order to send the message that you want and expect their participation. The Super-Pause is your way of telling the audience that participation

Offer a tip of the day, week or month

Offer a business improvement tip or a tip about health or safety issues. Provide a tip about where to dine out during the upcoming sales conference or about how the audience can present information more effectively. Make it a "to-do" tip or a "to-avoid" tip. Assign someone in the meeting the responsibility of providing the tip.

Add a special feature

A special feature segment is similar to the features you see on newscasts that relate to fitness, health, diet, business, family, community, professional development or current events. You can assign the special feature segment to a member of your team. This may or may not be information that is directly related to your topic, but it is of interest to your audience. It will help your audience to be able to do something better or be more informed about a topic.

If someone on your team is an exercise fanatic, let that person share a strategy for staying fit. Perhaps someone can share a process for setting and achieving personal and professional goals. Or have someone provide an executive summary about a book they have recently read.

The special feature segments should be short and to the point. There is no limit to the topics that can be covered in these segments. However, there should be a limit on the time you spend on the special feature segments, so be sure to set strict time allotments for these segments. Roughly 2 to 3 minutes should be plenty of time to cover these special feature topics. Make sure the person leading these segments practices and times the duration of the segment. Otherwise, the 3 minutes designated for this segment can easily turn into 10 minutes.

Invite a special guest

Schedule a guest for your meeting. Invite a customer, an expert in your industry, a local businessperson, a television personality or a coach. Contact a local university and ask the sports information director, marketing director or assistant athletic director to join you. Try to schedule an elected official or the president of a local triathlon or sailing club. Call your chamber of commerce and request a list of clubs and organizations in the area.

Keep the guest's time commitment to a minimum, and limit the amount of preparation work the guest will need to do. In other words, make it easy for the guest to contribute to your meeting. Have the guest provide a brief overview of the topic and then move directly to a question-and-answer session. The guest shouldn't be required to prepare a presentation, unless she has one that is ready to be delivered.

Do your homework. Ask the guest questions that tie into your theme. Ask questions that lead to lively and interesting discussions. Ask questions that will help the audience learn something new or something that will improve their life in some way.

Make the guest feel welcome. Follow up the guest appearance with a thank-you note for participating in the meeting. If possible, give her a token of your appreciation.

An enthusiastic effort to bring guests to your meetings will lead to a situation where your participants look forward to the "guest appearance" segment.

Be sure to consider how your ideas will play out with your particular audience. What seems like a bright idea prior to the meeting can backfire if it is not executed properly. The following blog entry is an example of how an excellent idea can go awry.

Blog entry from Phil in Dallas, Texas

I decided to inject some fun into my virtual meeting by

developing a masquerade party theme. All of the participants were to identify themselves as their favorite animated character from television. The meeting started out
great, lots of laughs as the various characters checked into
the meeting.

The characters started communicating with each other,
using the terminology their characters use on television.
At first, it was hilarious! As it continued, it became less
and less funny to me. I soon realized I had lost control of
the meeting. The participants who remained in character
had a great time. The other participants were frustrated
and annoyed by the whole concept. Nothing of value was
accomplished. I will not be conducting another virtual
masquerade party theme any time soon, or should I say
"ever."

VIRTUAL HUMOR

Using humor can be awkward when you can't see or hear the audience. You have to be exceedingly confident that your material is
funny. It tests your nerves to hear nothing but the beating of your
own heart after you uncork your most gut-busting line. The audience might be laughing hysterically at the other end of the connection, but on your end, the silence is deafening.

Create an environment in which people feel comfortable enough
to laugh. You may want to alert your audience that something you
are about to say is intended to be funny. For example, say:

"I hope we can have some fun during the presentation
today. Feel free to smile or laugh at anything you think is
intended to be funny."

"This is a serious business topic, but let's not lose our

sense of humor and our creativity as we work toward a solution."

"I saw something yesterday that made me laugh out loud. I was boarding my flight from Tampa when . . ."

"You will not believe what the guest speaker said at last week's conference . . ."

Blog entry from Joe in Newport Beach, California

I live in Southern California. A hotel in my neighborhood hosts a weekly comedy show. The person in charge of liquor sales at the hotel is the father of a friend of mine. The audiences are generally small, so a little laughter goes a long way in encouraging the audience to stay, enjoy the show and order drinks. My friend's dad made us an offer we couldn't refuse. If we would come to the comedy show every Thursday night and laugh enthusiastically at the jokes, he would provide free drinks for us throughout the show. What a deal!

It was interesting how much more the audience would laugh when the comedian had our support as a foundation on which to build her routine. We were the laugh track, so to speak, for the show. 💬

When you are using humor with an invisible and silent audience, and the audience can't see you, the audience doesn't have the ability to read your facial expressions or body language to gain nonverbal clues as to the intent of your words. Your vocal intonation, volume and pace must serve as their indicators that something different is coming their way.

Keep the humor relevant to the topic and the audience.

Telling a joke for the sake of telling a joke can be risky. If you link your humor to a message and they laugh, great. They enjoyed the humor, and they heard the message. If they don't laugh (or you can't hear them laugh), that's all right too. At least they heard the message.

> If your humor is relevant, appropriate and relates directly to your message, then it's OK whether they laugh or not. Either way, you have reinforced your message.

Participants can't always hear everything that is being said during a virtual presentation. If you are going to attempt humor, be sure that your audience can hear you. Any laughter, talking, paper shuffling or coughing will most likely drown out some of your words. Most of us have been on conference calls where we were remote, but a group of attendees was located in a single conference room. You couldn't hear what was being said, but you could hear everyone in the conference room laugh. You missed the humor. In most cases, humorous comments that are repeated are not as funny as when they were first stated. The humor loses its punch. Since most sound systems used during virtual presentations do not to allow multiple voices to be heard simultaneously, the one-liner that someone throws into the conversation is frequently not heard. The people in the room with the person using the one-liner can hear it, but the remote participants most likely cannot.

There are three basic rules for humor used in virtual presentations:

Rule #1: The humor must be appropriate. This same rule applies to humor used in face-to-face presentations. However, keep in mind that the chance that something will be misinterpreted or taken out of context during a virtual presentation is significantly higher than during face-to-face presentations.

Rule #2: It must be relevant to the topic or it should be left out of the presentation.

Rule #3: Virtual humor is harder to execute than face-to-face humor is, so be more selective about when you use it.

Being resourceful does not require you to create never-before-attempted tactics for your virtual presentations. Think outside the screen. There are countless ways to be resourceful. It's not about coming up with something completely new. It's about using the resources, talents and tools around you to make your presentation more dynamic. You don't need to dream up some new strategy or technique to make your presentation better. Find ideas that already exist. Modify them to meet your needs. And achieve better meeting results by building them into your presentations.

KEEP IT MOVING

Your virtual presentation must keep moving, or it will be abandoned.

THE PACE AND TIMING OF YOUR VIRTUAL PRESENTATION should be quicker than it is during your in-person presentations. I'm not suggesting that you talk faster. I'm suggesting that you establish a more upbeat tempo. You can't allow your virtual audience to become bored. You have fewer tools and techniques at your disposal to regain their attention.

All aspects of your virtual presentation must be efficient. As you prepare, think of every possible way to streamline your material.

CHAPTER 11
DON'T GET BOGGED DOWN, FOR ANY REASON

BE HYPEREFFICIENT WITH THE TIME ALLOTTED for your virtual presentation. Efficiency is an absolute must. The distractions for a remote audience are too tempting and too numerous to let your presentations drag. As soon as the audience starts losing interest in what you are saying or showing, their collective minds begin to wander.

If a snafu occurs during your in-person presentations, you have ways to keep your audience involved, such as having them talk among themselves, start a group discussion or take a quick break as you reboot. During a virtual presentation, it takes more effort to overcome the snafu and keep your audience from getting sidetracked. You have to get back on track quicker if you want the audience to stay with you.

ELIMINATE THE IRRELEVANT

Review your information several times, keeping an eye out for opportunities to streamline your message. If the information doesn't add sizzle to your presentation, strengthen your message, drive home an important point or otherwise make your presentation more interesting, eliminate it. Throw everything off the boat that is not essential to keeping it afloat and keeping it moving toward its destination.

PRACTICE YOUR DELIVERY

Nothing is more important than practicing your presentation. Throughout my book *The Exceptional Presenter*, I stated that everyday situations offer multiple opportunities to practice the various skill sets that are critical to presenting effectively. Repetition of skills, practiced the right way, will enable you to develop a consistent, strong, high-impact delivery.

> Those who practice improve; those who don't, don't.

Prior to the start of my daughter's ballet recital a couple of years back, the person in charge of the performance spoke to the audience. She works with professional ballet performers as well as my daughter's amateur group. She explained that prior to a performance the cast will practice for 6 weeks, 6 days a week, for 8 hours a day. By doing so, the performers develop the muscle memory needed to perform at the highest level.

Practice using the technology and the tools you will be using during your virtual presentation. Practice delivering your message out loud. Record your practice sessions. One of the benefits of the technology being used for online presentations is that you can record practice sessions and then review and critique the recordings.

Practice every part of your presentation. If you are presenting with other people, arrange practice sessions for your team. These team practice sessions are critical if you are going to execute effectively when you go live. Focus not only on the individual segments but also on your timing, the transitions and the handoffs. Get familiar with the information that your copresenters are going to cover, how their segments start and how they end.

During the practice sessions you can determine who and what will be on the screen, who will control the technology and how best to transition from person to person and from subject to subject.

In addition to practicing as a team, each presenter owes it to the team to work on his or her part individually. Be sure to note the amount of time each segment takes to complete. Do this every time you practice.

If the use of a particular tool is clumsy or awkward, don't use it until you have mastered it. By "mastering it," I mean that you are proficient with it and it does not distract you. Repetition is the best way to master the use of any of the tools.

MANAGE THE CLOCK

Managing the clock has not traditionally been the hallmark of most meeting leaders. This is especially true of virtual meetings. Meetings start late, time slips away, segments run overtime and drop-dead ending times are trampled over. It's not that presenters don't mean to stay on time; they just get lost in their material. Their internal clock is out of sync with real time.

Display a timer on the screen to keep your presentation on time. Determine how the host can signal the other presenters as to how much time is remaining. Respect the time of your audience. If you develop a reputation of being someone who starts and ends on time, if not early, participants are more likely to stay focused for the duration of your presentation.

Blog entry from Jane in Chicago, Illinois

Our team was preparing to deliver a virtual proposal. The prospect was brought to us by two of our New York agents, who insisted on being a part of the proposal team. It soon became apparent that the NY guys weren't planning to rehearse with us before the proposal.

Our team had practiced the presentation, start to finish, at least a dozen times, and we felt great about the content, flow and energy. Our NY guys refused to run through their parts, which happened to be the first two parts of the presentation. One said he would only need 2 minutes and that he is better off-the-cuff. The other insisted that he needed no more than 4 minutes. We had 45 minutes for our presentation and 15 additional minutes for Q&A. These were hard-and-fast time parameters.

Presentation day arrived. NY #1 started the presentation with his off-the-cuff opening remarks. As you might expect, his 2-minute opening ended up being a 6-minute opening. NY #2's 4-minute segment lasted 8 minutes. We were 14 minutes into a 45-minute presentation and had not even started our prepared remarks. We now had to cut 8 minutes out of the presentation because the NY guys didn't think they needed to practice. If I could have reached through cyberspace and slapped them, I would have. They didn't add any value to the presentation. 💬

The key take away from Jane's blog is that if someone refuses to practice with the team, that person should not be on the team.

The team that practices together, presents better.

As they say, you play like you practice. If your team practices, you will know what to expect during the presentation. If your team doesn't practice, you get what you deserve—a less than exceptional performance.

Getting bogged down while delivering a virtual presentation is the equivalent of being interrupted by a fire drill during an in-person presentation. The difference is that during a fire drill, people physically leave the building, whereas during a virtual presentation, they mentally flee the area.

CHAPTER 12
CREATE SEAMLESS TRANSITIONS

FOR YOUR MEETINGS TO FLOW SEAMLESSLY, your transitions must be efficient and succinct. Well-executed transitions will prevent many of the uncomfortable moments that occur as a result of presenters, or the audience, not knowing what is supposed to happen next. What should be a simple handoff to the next presenter can turn into a clumsy, hesitant and stalled moment in the presentation. Despite your best efforts, some of these moments are going to happen because of the technology being used and our inability to hear multiple voices simultaneously. But with planning and practice, nearly all of your transitions can be seamless.

You can use several techniques to ensure more efficient transitions. First, determine the transition that will take place between presenters. Let each presenter know his or her position on the agenda. Whenever possible, predetermine the transitions that will occur from one presenter to the next. For example, Pete should know that Theresa will transition to him. Both Pete and Theresa should know what transition Theresa will use. Pete should also know that when he is finished presenting he will transition to Tom. Likewise, Pete should let Tom know what transition he will use.

Second, determine how you are going to introduce team members, guests and topics during the presentation. Here are a few suggestions:

- When introducing a team member for the first time, include the experience that the person brings to the presentation, his or her expertise on the topic, the topic that will be covered and the purpose of the presentation.

- When introducing a guest, include information regarding the professional experience of the guest, the topic, the purpose of the presentation and the relevance of the information to the audience.

- When introducing a topic, include the name and title of the person presenting the topic, the presenter's qualifications, the relevance of the topic to the audience and the amount of time that will be devoted to the topic.

Third, find a consistent way of signaling that one person has completed his comment and that he is turning the microphone over to someone else. This is especially important in a free-flowing conversation when transitions are more difficult. Transitions used in the broadcasting industry (discussed in chapter 2, "Virtual Presentations Are Anything but New") will come in handy in these situations. For instance, "Cathy, that appears to be our best course of action at this time. With that I will turn it over to Chris who will provide the data that backs up our conclusion, Chris." Or, "That appears to be the best course of action at this time. Thanks, Cathy. Now Chris will provide the data . . ."

Keep your transitions simple.

When you have multiple participants, it becomes your responsibility to control the flow of the conversations, the comments and, to some extent, the transitions. There are times when you will have to "cut off" someone because that person doesn't know how or when to stop talking.

If you are leading the meeting, think like a radio or television talk show host. In order to take questions and comments from callers, the host must be efficient getting the callers on the line and getting them off the line. Getting them off the line is an important skill that requires tact because many of the people who call into these shows will continue to talk until they are cut off. Some callers have a difficult time getting to the point. Other callers ask questions that are not relevant to the topic at hand.

When taking a call or dropping a call, be efficient and be professional.

In: "Jim, in region 4, you have a question for our panelists?"

Out: "Jim, thanks for your question. Now let's move on to . . ."

In: "Julie is calling with a question about the new compensation package. Julie, specifically what would you like to know?"

Out: "This information is relevant for everyone on this call. Thanks, Julie. Here is a follow-up to Julie's question . . ."

Be efficient when transitioning from one person to another: "Carol, thanks for your comment. Jim, in San Diego, how do you feel about the changes we've outlined?"

Other methods of creating seamless transitions include, but are not limited to, the following:

- Provide a visual signal on the screen that alerts the host that someone is about to make a comment. If you are in the same room as someone making a comment, decide on a few simple hand signals that indicate an upcoming transition.

- State the next person's name during the last sentence of your comment to alert the person that you are turning it over to him.

- Delineate the segments so that it is clear when one segment is over and you are moving on to another segment. "That concludes our discussion of the Acme account. Next, let's turn it over to Sally and Matt in Cincinnati who will provide a review of the new zoning laws and their impact on our growth projections."

You know your audience. Use whatever you think will work for them.

If the audience members are not familiar with each other, then be sure to provide a name and possibly a title every time someone joins the conversation. If you are in a virtual meeting with multiple participants, it is difficult to distinguish the voices, especially when you are not familiar with all of the people on the call.

Host: "Now we'll hear from our National Accounts Manager, Steve Jones. Steve."

Participant: "This is Michelle, Vice President of sales in Boston. I want to make a comment regarding . . ."

Michelle's next comment should start with something like:

"This is Michelle in Boston again, with a question about ..."

Make your transitions efficient. The more efficient they are, the stronger the bond will be from one topic to the next. Seamless transitions will help to make your virtual presentations sound professional. They will make you appear more organized. And seamless transitions make it easier for the audience to follow the flow of information.

CHAPTER 13
FOLLOW UP

FOLLOWING UP A MEETING IS always important, but it is probably more important after a virtual presentation than it is after an in-person presentation. When you are in the same room as your audience, you have greater control of the flow of information, your interaction with the participants and what is handed out to them. You have the advantage of seeing the facial expressions and body language that help you assess everyone's understanding of the topic. The participants are also more likely to speak up if they are confused, lost or skeptical about what is being discussed. It is more difficult for a participant to "jump into" a virtual conversation because of the technology and the remote aspects of the conversation. Therefore, some people will choose to keep quiet and not rock the boat or take a chance by speaking up.

Remember that participants have become accustomed to multitasking during virtual presentations. If they are multitasking, they most likely are not hearing a significant amount of detail. They might hear it, but it probably isn't registering below a surface level. The Stanford study on multitasking reaffirmed that multitaskers can't assimilate multiple streams of information simultaneously. They don't organize incoming information effectively and can't filter irrelevant information. They constantly scan for new information and tend not to ponder the information they possess.

Therefore, we have to be more thorough in providing follow-up material that the participants can use to review and gain additional insights.

DO IT NOW

Send the follow-up material as soon as possible. The longer you wait to send it, the less likely it is to be reviewed and the less impact the information will have. Give your participants the chance to act on it while it is fresh in their mind.

STREAMLINE THE INFORMATION

Send a single package, email or document. Don't have each presenter send summary material separately. Sending multiple summaries from multiple sources is ineffective. It will frustrate your participants and minimize the benefits of the follow-up material.

When there are multiple presenters involved in a meeting, one person should be assigned the task of gathering all of the follow-up material into one document. Anyone who presented during the meeting should provide a brief summary of their presentation. For panel discussions, assign someone the task of taking notes and summarizing the discussion points. This summary should also be included as part of the follow-up material.

The follow-up material should not include every detail. It doesn't make sense to send an overwhelming amount of follow-up material. The participants won't have time to review it all.

You committed to respect the participants' time during the presentation. Commit to respect their time with the follow-up material as well.

Provide a summary of the presentation material, the decisions that were made and the key take-away points. Include the specific action steps that need to be taken. Clearly identify who will take these action steps. Set specific dates and times for the action steps to be taken and completed.

Determine who needs to see this information. How much detail you include in the follow-up material will depend on your audience and your topic.

Include directions and links to additional information and resources. If the presentation was recorded, provide your participants with the instructions needed to view it online.

Most of the information going into the summary package can be prepared prior to the presentation. It's easier to create the follow-up material as you organize the presentation. When the presentation is over, you want to move on with your life and not have to spend time getting your summary material together.

Providing your participants with a well-organized and succinct packet of follow-up material is the professional thing to do. Your follow-up material should provide a review of the presentation. It should be a resource for the participants to learn more about the topics. And it should be in their possession as soon after the presentation as possible.

CHAPTER 14
TO GO VIRTUAL OR NOT TO GO VIRTUAL

WHAT SHOULD YOU CONSIDER when making the decision to deliver your presentation face-to-face, to present your information virtually or to use a combination of the two? Your choice should be based on what will give you the best result for the presentation objectives that you have established.

Virtual is often the preferred option when the primary considerations are the urgency in communicating the message, geographic location(s) of the audience, flexibility of timing, efficiency and costs (such as airfare, ground transportation, hotel, meals, cab fares, meeting rooms and parking). Online communication tools offer incredible savings of time and money. They offer the opportunity to connect with people at great distances with whom you would otherwise not connect. With virtual presentations, your reach is almost limitless. Virtual presentations offer an array of technology to make your meetings exciting and multidimensional.

Virtual presentations also provide an opportunity for corporations to demonstrate their commitment to the environment. Less travel by employees means less impact on the environment. This translates to a smaller carbon footprint, which can help companies meet their "green" objectives.

Based on several studies, referenced later in this chapter, virtual presentations are the favored venue when the presentation involves information dissemination and data presentation. Virtual presentations are also favored when there is a limited amount of time to get the information to the target audience.

Think about virtual presentations this way. Virtual presentations can provide an extra layer of connectivity and a broader level of intimacy with your customers that you would not be able to get otherwise. They offer an opportunity to make contact with key accounts multiple times to share with them information that will add value to their business.

Virtual presentations also give you more opportunities to influence the customer and provide insights, advice and solutions. You can almost instantaneously put your customers in touch with a leading expert or specialist who can help find solutions to their most immediate and pressing issues.

In the time it takes your competitor to set up a meeting, fly from San Francisco to New York, stay the night at a hotel and take a cab to the customer's office, you have already met with that customer virtually and resolved their issue.

Face-to-face presentations are currently preferred for building relationships with coworkers or clients, closing the deal, building consensus, networking, sharing ideas and making decisions. They're also optimal when more complex strategic thinking is required.

As you make your decision to meet face-to-face, to meet virtually or to use a combination of the two, don't forget about the intangible benefits of looking someone in the eye, shaking hands, having a glass of wine over dinner or having conversations that might not happen during your virtual connections.

Virtual meetings offer many benefits, but they are not, as of yet, the preferred and most effective means of communication and relationship building. It makes more sense to think of virtual presentations as a supplement to, not as a replacement for, in-person contact with your customers, prospects, employees, vendors and users.

> As people become more comfortable and competent using virtual presentation tools, the preference for face-to-face presentations will begin to decline.

When considering whether to conduct your presentation virtually, face-to-face or a combination of the two, think about the following scenario:

Blog entry from Mike in Washington, DC

I am the CEO of an online consulting business. We scheduled a meeting to try to finalize a contract with a major prospect. I was joining the meeting remotely, but one of my managers was at the meeting. After the meeting, my manager called me and said that the decision maker looked uneasy toward the end of the meeting. My manager couldn't put his finger on it, but said that the decision maker, "Just didn't seem comfortable with how the meeting ended." Upon hearing this, I called the decision maker and found out that she was indeed uncomfortable with how the meeting ended and that she didn't like one of the terms in the contract. Why the decision maker didn't verbalize her concern during the meeting, we didn't know.

What I did know is that I needed to schedule a get-together as soon as possible. Fortunately, I was able to meet with her the next morning for coffee. This less formal follow-up conversation gave me the opportunity to clarify two important points in the contract. The decision maker's comfort level improved during our coffee talk, and we are now partnering on a significant project. I never did find out why she didn't state her concerns during the virtual meeting. But all is now good, and we have established a strong working relationship. 💬

Had his employee not been in the room and sensed the discomfort, Mike never would have suspected that there was an issue. He would not have scheduled the follow-up conversation and might not have earned the business. Mike later said: "The prospect was making a choice of vendors by the end of the week. The issue in contention, unless resolved, could have lost us a significant piece of business. I'm sure if I had been at the meeting, I would have picked up on her body language. Luckily, we had a manager in the room who did pick up on it."

Several years ago, United Airlines ran a commercial in which a sales team was sitting around a conference table looking glum. The company had just lost a big account to a competitor. Everyone in the room was anticipating a verbal beat-down by the boss. But instead of delivering a tirade, the boss walked around the room and hand delivered airline tickets to each salesperson. The tickets were to be used to go see their existing clients, face-to-face, and reaffirm their commitment to those clients.

There are no hard-and-fast rules for determining when to present virtually or face-to-face. Each situation needs to be assessed to determine the smartest (not necessarily the cheapest) way to achieve your desired objective or result.

VIRTUAL PRESENTATIONS VS. FACE-TO-FACE

When considering whether to conduct your presentation virtually or face-to-face or to use a combination of the two, consider the circumstances. Put an "X" in the column by the one *you* would prefer for each of the situations in the following table:

Situation	Virtual*	Face-to-face	Combination
1. You need to communicate your message to a geographically dispersed audience.			
2. The situation is urgent and the word needs to get out quickly.			
3. You want to close the deal.			
4. You want to develop a relationship with prospective new clients.			
5. You need to negotiate an important contract with a client.			
6. You want to brainstorm solutions to a problem with your staff.			
7. You need input from others to help you make a difficult decision.			

* The term includes teleconferences, videoconferences and web conferences.

Situation	Virtual*	Face-to-face	Combination
8. You need to persuade your client to purchase your product or service.			
9. You want to save travel time for yourself and for others.			
10. You need to save money due to a reduced travel budget.			
11. You need to call a meeting on short notice with people in multiple locations.			
12. Interaction with others is needed for complex strategic thinking.			
13. You need to present the data from a customer satisfaction survey to customer service managers at all locations.			
14. You are interviewing senior staff for key positions.			
15. A client contacts you and seems to be very upset about a "potentially costly issue" that has just arisen.			

TANGIBLE AND INTANGIBLE COSTS AND BENEFITS

The tangible savings of a virtual presentation can be calculated immediately. How can you measure the intangible factors? Face-

* The term includes teleconferences, videoconferences and web conferences.

to-face meetings offer a multitude of opportunities for people to run into each other and start a spontaneous conversation. Think about all of the places you can generate a conversation with someone that can lead to a relationship, a follow-up meeting, a conversation or a lead.

During the course of a 1-day or a 2-day conference, I have developed business relationships with people based on a chance meeting in every one of the following places. How about you?

- At the airport waiting for a flight. You might even be traveling as a team to the conference. In this case you could have 3 to 4 hours of travel time together to not only discuss business but also to learn more about the people with whom you are traveling.
- While on the flight to or coming back from the conference
- Waiting for your luggage
- Riding on the shuttle to or from the conference center or hotel
- Checking in at the hotel
- Walking through a lobby or the hallways at the conference
- Standing in line at the conference registration desk
- Taking a refreshment break
- Waiting for a breakout workshop or keynote session to begin
- At a networking function
- At the hotel bar
- During breakfast, lunch or dinner
- In the workout room early in the morning or at the completion of the day's events
- During a team building event
- In the elevator

It would be unusual *not to run into* someone in these places during a 1- or 2-day conference.

Many meaningful connections happen during these spontaneous, relaxed, conversational and chance interactions. Most of these chance connections are nonexistent when your meetings occur online. They just are not part of the process. The logistics don't allow for them to take place.

I recently conducted a workshop at a national sales conference in Dallas. After my session, I was checking email and getting some work finished at a table outside the meeting room. The day was over except for a dinner that was to begin an hour later. There was a group of eight sales managers from different regions of the country sitting around a table. They were engrossed in a business conversation for at least 45 minutes. When I left to go back to my room, they were still there having a lively discussion. Contacts were made, best practices were shared and camaraderie was built.

That group discussion would not have happened virtually. It wasn't planned. They all just happened to be sitting at a couple of adjoining tables and fell into a conversation. If your virtual meeting took place in a high-tech telepresence room, you couldn't hang around chatting with each other for an hour after the meeting. The next group scheduled to use the room would kick you out.

Sometimes the benefits of face-to-face presentations extend to more than just conversations that are created when you get people together. Seeing someone across the room at a social function can trigger an idea or thought or it might remind you to get in touch with that person. Or using that *give-me-a-call* gesture can generate a connection or conversation in the days or weeks that follow the conference.

If the primary objective for conducting your presentation virtually is to save time and money, you need to look carefully to find out the cost of conducting these meetings online instead of face-to-face.

If your virtual presentations and meetings are ineffective, then you haven't gained a thing. The money you saved by restricting travel and limiting your face-to-face meeting time with clients, employees and prospects is potentially dwarfed by the money you lost because your message didn't get across, you failed to connect with the prospect or you were unable to build rapport and secure a relationship. Be careful that you are not winning the battle (saving time and money) but losing the war (damaging internal and external relationships). Are you achieving short-term gains while losing your long-term focus? Are you sacrificing significant revenue for the sake of saving a few dollars in the short term?

Blog entry from James in Silicon Valley, California

Our Fortune 100 company spent $3,000 per participant for last year's in-person global sales conference. Multiply $3,000 by 3,000 employees, and we ended up shelling out a cool $9,000,000 for the conference. It's easy to see the attraction of conducting this year's conference online. The cost per attendee at this year's online conference was roughly $600 per participant, and our expenditure for the entire conference was a grand total of $1,800,000. We saved $7,200,000 by taking our conference online. We would have to find some pretty impressive intangibles to make up for $7.2 million dollars. 💬

Some of the impact of your online meeting can only be measured over a longer term. What if your competitor is getting face-to-face with the CEO of your best customer, but you're not? The smile, the handshake, the casual conversation could turn the tide in favor of your competitor.

Sometimes the hardest thing about a face-to-face meeting is getting face-to-face.

In the "War for Talent," are you recruiting your top prospects by phone, email or virtual interviews exclusively? No way! You want to make them feel welcome. You want them to experience your culture. You want to treat them like family. You want to make it personal.

If you say you are committed to the development and retention of your people, yet you have cut all travel, off-site meetings and training, are you truly living up to your commitment? Your people probably don't think so.

TOOL OR CRUTCH?

During the 2009 and 2010 health-care debates, many public officials opened the lines of communication to their constituents by conducting Town Hall meetings. Some of these meetings were marked by heated exchanges, shouting and frustration.

Some representatives, seeing how hotly contested these meetings were becoming, decided to conduct their Town Hall meetings online. These were called Tele-Town Hall meetings. By doing so, these officials could say they were willing to meet with their constituents and at the same time demonstrate they were not technological dinosaurs.

Their real reason for taking their Town Hall meetings online seemed obvious. By conducting meetings in this way, they could control every aspect of them: They could mute the audience, thus eliminating the dissenting voices. They could pick and choose the questions they were most comfortable answering and avoid the difficult questions. Heck, for that matter, they could even make up their own questions. They could answer questions without interruption and take as long as they wished to answer them.

These Tele-Town Hall meetings were much more "civil" than the in-person ones. But did they serve their purpose? Although they were called Tele-Town Halls, as far as providing a way for constituents to ask questions and express their opinions they were more like Teletubby Town Halls. Everyone was happy. There was no dissension. There were no raised voices. Elected officials could take questions from audience members who were friendly toward their position on a given issue and keep everyone else muted. They could have an army of assistants searching for and providing responses to the various questions.

Not a whole lot was accomplished during these Teletubby Town Halls, but that's all right; the elected officials gave their constituents what they were looking for—a Town Hall meeting. The politicians could check it off their "things to do" list.

When choosing whether to conduct your meeting, Q & A session or "town hall" in person or online, consider these questions: Are you making the decision to go online because it is the most effective and efficient means of communicating with your audience? Or does going online provide a crutch so you can check the box while not having to contend with the difficult issues?

A confident presenter will choose the venue that is more effective, even if it is the more difficult choice to execute.

Are you using virtual meetings as a tool or as a crutch? Is your virtual meeting a signal to your customer that she is on the B-list? "We would love to get together with you, but our budget cutbacks are forcing us to only meet face-to-face with our most important customers. When the economy bounces back, we'll get together with you again."

Did you damage a relationship because you were not face-to-face? Or did you make a positive statement about the value of your relationship by making the effort to meet in person? After all, your customer doesn't care how much money you are saving. Your customer wants to know how you are going to grow her company's bottom line.

WHAT THE STUDIES TELL US

It is important to note some of the research that sheds light on the financial implications and consequences of your choice to present face-to-face, to go virtual or to use a combination of the two. Keeping this research in mind can help you approach your decision with a broader perspective and a clearer understanding of the current preferences.

According to the Oxford Economic April 2009 report (sponsored by the U.S. Travel Association)

- More than 75 percent of customers either require or prefer in-person meetings.
- Among business travelers across all industries, 25 percent of existing customers and 28 percent of revenue could be

lost to competitors if customers were not met in person. Corporate executives said that 28 percent of their business would be lost without in-person meetings.

- Both executives and business travelers estimate that roughly 40 percent of their prospective customers are converted to new customers with an in-person meeting compared to 16 percent without such a meeting.

- For every dollar invested in business travel, companies realize $12.50 in incremental revenue.

Referring once again to the August 2009 *Forbes Insights* article "Business Meetings—The Case for Face-to-Face," the survey findings revealed that 59 percent of the 750 executives surveyed had increased their use of technology-driven meetings during the recession. More than one-third said they were traveling much less than before the recession. More than eight out of ten respondents, however, still preferred face-to-face meetings for building relationships; being better able to read body language and facial expressions; enhancing social interaction; being able to bond with coworkers and clients; allowing more complex strategic thinking; and providing a better environment for tough, timely decision making.

The executives who preferred virtual meetings did so for reasons such as saving time, saving money, being more flexible in the location and timing of the meeting, increasing productivity and allowing opportunities to multitask.

The study also asked executives which meeting method is most conducive to fostering key business actions, attributes and outcomes effectively. Face-to-face meetings are preferred at least sevenfold for persuasion, leadership, engagement, inspiration, decision making, accountability, candor, focus, clarity, brainstorming, strategizing and reaching consensus.

The preference shifts in favor of virtual meetings when the meeting involves data presentation and information dissemination and when the meeting is urgent.

A September 2009 *Harvard Business Review* study of 2,300 business leaders from the United States, Europe and Asia found that

- 79 percent view in-person meetings as a highly effective way to meet new clients and to sell business.
- 87 percent agree that face-to-face meetings are essential to "sealing the deal."
- 95 percent agree that face-to-face meetings are key to building long-term relationships.

The leaders in the *Harvard Business Review* study see face-to-face meetings as more effective for

- Negotiating important contracts.
- Interviewing senior staff for key positions.
- Understanding and listening to important customers.

I bring this information to your attention to help you determine the right choice, face-to-face or virtual, for your meeting or presentation. These studies highlight the idea that virtual meetings offer many benefits, but they are not, as of yet, the preferred and most effective means of communication and relationship building. It makes more sense to think of virtual presentations as a supplement to, not a replacement for, in-person presentations.

There is a lot to consider when making your choice of virtual, face-to-face or a combination of the two. To help make your decision, look at the big picture. By doing so, you will be more confident with your decision and you will select the venue that is most conducive to conducting a meeting that achieves your objective.

"Since we all agree, let's finalize the contract."

By employing exceptional presentation skills, the desired results of your virtual meetings will more closely mirror the results of your face-to-face meetings.

CHAPTER 15
THE VIRTUAL BEGINNING

THIS ISN'T THE CONCLUSION. THIS IS THE BEGINNING. I can't end a book about virtual presentations with a "conclusion." Virtual presentations are in their infancy. This is the starting point to broaden your communication reach, refine your presentation delivery skills in any venue and have total confidence that your message is well crafted, clear and compelling.

I hope that this book will enable you to maximize your impact using any virtual presentation technology. Instead of dreading virtual presentations and meetings, I'm confident that you will thrive in this environment.

Challenge yourself and your team to establish higher standards and expectations for your virtual presentations.

The technology driving these presentations will continue to evolve. The connections will become easier, the quality of sound and video will improve and the tools at your disposal will expand and become simpler to use.

But none of the technology can replace the impact you will have on your audience by keeping everything in your presentation relevant, keeping everything you do during your presentation engaging, and keeping your presentation moving.

It's not about the technology. It's about how you structure and deliver your message using the technology. You must carry the message.

Now, go spread your message to all parts of the planet. Have fun. And BE EXCEPTIONAL!

VIRTUAL PRESENTATION FORMS

(All of these forms can be downloaded at www.theexceptional presenter.com.)

VIRTUAL PREP SHEET

NAME: TIME:
MEETING NAME: DATE:

"The purpose (or objective/mission/goal) of my presentation today is to . . .

_____

_____."

"If you remember only one (two, three) point(s) from this presentation,
remember this . . .

_____

_____

_____."

"The agenda for this presentation includes . . . (This must be brief, less than 30
seconds.)

_____

_____

_____."

"The situation is as follows" OR "We are positioned as follows . . .

_____

_____."

"The end result (consequence/ramification/benefit) is . . .

_____

_____."

"The next step(s) is to . . .

_____

_____."

End the presentation with a purpose statement: "I'd like you to leave here
remembering one important point . . .

_____

_____."

CONTENT

1) What topics will I cover and in what sequence, considering "Most important first"?

_____   _____   _____

2) How deep do I need to go with each topic?

3) How much time for discussion or Q&A?

4) What resources can I use to prepare?

DELIVERY

Method?

What tools are available?

Can I manage the tools alone, or do I need assistance?

       Who will fill the role of producer?

       Who will provide tech support?

Who else should be involved in the presentation? What role?

Name: Role: Assignment:

Name: Role: Assignment:

TO DO
- Complete the Sequencing Chart
- Get participant list, locations and local times
- Send a copy of the meeting agenda to all participants
- Send meeting expectations and info regarding anything they need to prepare or think about
-
-

FOLLOW-UP
- Who will be responsible for coordinating follow-up?
- Provide summary of presentation, support material, web links and contact information
- Send presentation evaluations
-
-

SEQUENCING CHART Timing, Topics, Talent, Tools and Transitions

Name of presentation or meeting: _____

Role: _____ **Technology:** _____

Segment objectives: _____

Topics to cover: _____

Time	Topic	Talent (Who?) and Tools (What will be used?)	Transition Used

ROLE GUIDELINES

Meeting: _____ Date: _____

Time: _____ Meeting type: _____

Person: _____ Role: _____

Topic: _____

Segment objective: _____

_____

Time allotment: _____

Provided for you: _____

_____

Follow-up: _____

_____

Additional information and suggestions: _____

_____

_____

Keep it relevant. Keep it engaging. Keep it moving.
- Take pride in your segment.
- Do not exceed your allotted time.
- Practice improves: confidence, content, delivery and timing.

ACKNOWLEDGMENTS

TO CHERYL DRAKE, editor extraordinaire. You had your work cut out for you once again. Thanks for your professionalism and your outstanding guidance throughout the process of developing this book. Contact Cheryl at cheryldrake@sbcglobal.net.

To the talented and funny Tom Holtkamp. Your illustrations are spot on. To see more of Tom's work visit www.tomholtkamp.com.

To the team at Greenleaf Book Group. Great work as usual.

FOR MORE INFORMATION, ideas and resources to improve your presentation skills visit:

www.theexceptionalpresenter.com

- Download the preparation sheets and assessment forms.
- Preview audio and video clips.
- Peruse our client list.
- Link to other resources.
- See what others are saying about, and how they are applying the techniques in, *The Exceptional Presenter Goes Virtual.*

ABOUT THE AUTHOR

TIM KOEGEL is a *New York Times* and *Wall Street Journal* best-selling author. Tim is the founder of the Presentation Academy, which offers individual, group and team presentation training. The academy also offers proposal preparation, CEO boot camps and a range of certification and licensing programs.

Tim's techniques are being applied around the world. His book *The Exceptional Presenter: A Proven Formula to OPEN UP! and Own the Room* has been published in multiple languages. His techniques are being taught at some of America's premier business schools and Fortune 1000 companies.

Tim has conducted workshops at the White House, for members of the United States Senate and House of Representatives and at the Department of Defense.

He is in high demand as a keynote speaker at corporate and association conferences.

is mandatory and you are willing to wait them out. It is a powerful signal that you are in control of the presentation.

After you have requested a response and you have paused, say something that alerts the audience that you are going to speak again. For example, say: "If there are no questions or comments at this time (Pause again for 2–4 seconds to make sure someone hasn't starting talking but you can't hear them) . . . let's move on to . . ." By adding this shorter pause, you can avoid stepping on the words of the person who asks a question or makes a comment.

MAKE YOUR PRESENTATION A *MUST-SEE* EVENT

By being resourceful, you can develop a reputation as someone who possesses exceptional virtual presentation skills and someone whose presentations can't be missed.

Here are a dozen ideas that you can use or modify to make your virtual presentation one that people will want to attend.

Assign roles

Assigning roles to your participants creates instant participation. You don't have to stick with the roles outlined in this book. Create your own set of roles, depending on the personalities and responsibilities in your organization. Just be sure the roles are appropriate for your meeting.

Rotate the roles

If your meetings regularly involve the same participants, rotate their roles. You can use the forms in this book to provide each role player everything necessary to be well prepared to carry out their role. Encourage each person who is assuming a role to present something interesting, thought provoking, unique, entertaining or humorous. And remind them to bring their enthusiasm.

The more interesting the topic is to the people delivering the information, the more enthusiastic they will be as they present it.

Share stories and examples that relate to the topic

Whatever story you choose to tell during your online presentation, make sure it is directly related to the topic and that it is succinct. Get to the point quickly. You can lose the attention of the audience if the story seems to have no end or if it is not interesting to the meeting participants. Stories consume time. Use them, but use them judiciously.

If you plan to add a story, practice it several times before the presentation. Find ways to shorten it without losing the point. Tell the story to several people so you can see how they react to it. If you tell a story to someone, you will immediately sense if it will support your point or if it will simply fill time.

Vary your openings

Don't begin your presentations the same way every time. Vary your opening remarks. Use a quote, a fact, a current event or a humorous story. Start with an audio or video clip that will grab the attention of your audience. Do as the newscasts do—go directly to a report by a remote member of the audience.

Create some competition

Create some type of competition to generate energy and enthusiasm for your presentations.

It is amazing what happens to people when they have a chance to compete. I recently attended a half-day webinar where the participants were divided into teams for the duration of the meeting. Teams were awarded points for everything from being in the meeting on time, to answering questions, to the best team presentations. The teams faced a deduction of points for such things as being late, not following directions and lack of effort.

The reward was a $100 gift certificate for each team member on the winning team and a $50 gift certificate for each team member of the second-place team. It was remarkable how hard the teams worked during the session. I don't think the dollar amount was as important to them as working together to capture first place. It was not the size of the winning purse that mattered. It was the thrill of victory that they sought. It was the agony of defeat that they wanted to avoid. The friendly competition drew the teams together and created some peer pressure to work hard throughout the meeting for the benefit of the team.

Reward participation

Think of all the money you are saving, in travel costs, by conducting your presentations virtually. Share a percentage of that savings with your audience. Reward things such as

- Participation.
- Comments, insights and ideas.
- Someone taking a risk or stepping up to take charge.
- Answers to questions about your products, customer service, competitors and market conditions, or for information communicated during the meeting.
- Leadership.
- The work the presenters did in preparing for the presentation.

Recognize effort

Provide recognition often. Who doesn't appreciate being recognized for an accomplishment? Make it a habit to recognize meeting participants for things they have achieved or are working hard to accomplish. Recognize them for a great effort. Recognize them for something they are involved with outside of the business (for example, chairing a not-for-profit organization, competing in a triathlon, or attending the graduation of a son or daughter from college).

Use games trainers play

Adapt a training game for your meetings. There are a number of "Games Trainers Play" books available that cover various ideas you can include in your presentations. Some of these games can help break the ice and break up the monotony of a meeting.

Whenever you are considering using a game, be sure that it is appropriate, that it adds a quality element to the meeting and that it does not simply add time to the length of the meeting. Some of these games, if conducted ineffectively, can feel hokey or contrived. They can be awkward for the participants and can eat up chunks of time that would be better spent on the topic at hand.

It's worth the price of purchasing a couple of the "Games Trainers Play" books to flip through and see how you can modify or adapt some of the exercises to your audience.

Trivia, anyone?

Pose trivia questions to the participants. Again, select trivia questions that are related to the topic of your presentation. Perhaps it is a question that will be answered at some point during the presentation. The only way they can know the answer is to pay attention.